# CONTENTS

Preface 7
by John Wilders

Introduction to *The Two Gentlemen of Verona* 9
by John Wilders

The Production 19
by Henry Fenwick

The BBC TV Cast and Production Team 30

The Text 32
with notes by Don Taylor

Glossary 90
by Geoffrey Miles

THE BBC TV SHAKESPEARE
Literary Consultant: John Wilders

THE TWO GENTLEMEN OF VERONA

# THE BBC TV SHAKESPEARE

ALL'S WELL THAT ENDS WELL
ANTONY AND CLEOPATRA
AS YOU LIKE IT
THE COMEDY OF ERRORS
CORIOLANUS
CYMBELINE
HAMLET
HENRY IV Part 1
HENRY IV Part 2
HENRY V
HENRY VI Part 1
HENRY VI Part 2
HENRY VI Part 3
HENRY VIII
JULIUS CAESAR
KING LEAR
MACBETH
MEASURE FOR MEASURE
THE MERCHANT OF VENICE
THE MERRY WIVES OF WINDSOR
A MIDSUMMER NIGHT'S DREAM
OTHELLO
PERICLES
RICHARD II
RICHARD III
ROMEO AND JULIET
THE TAMING OF THE SHREW
THE TEMPEST
TIMON OF ATHENS
TROILUS AND CRESSIDA
TWELFTH NIGHT
THE TWO GENTLEMEN OF VERONA
THE WINTER'S TALE

THE BBC TV SHAKESPEARE

Literary Consultant: John Wilders
Fellow of Worcester College, Oxford

# The Two Gentlemen of Verona

BRITISH BROADCASTING CORPORATION

Published by the
British Broadcasting Corporation
35 Marylebone High Street
London W1M 4AA

ISBN 0 563 20277 7

This edition first published 1984
© The British Broadcasting Corporation
and the Contributors 1984

The text of the Works of Shakespeare
edited by Peter Alexander
© William Collins Sons and Company Ltd 1951

The text of *The Two Gentlemen of Verona* used in this volume is the
Alexander text, edited by the late Professor Alexander and chosen by the
BBC as the basis for its television production, and is reprinted by
arrangement with William Collins Sons and Company Ltd. The complete
Alexander text is published in one volume by William Collins Sons and
Company Ltd under the title *The Alexander Text of the Complete Works of
William Shakespeare*.

All photographs are BBC copyright

Printed in Great Britain at
The Pitman Press, Bath

# PREFACE

## John Wilders

We do not know precisely when Shakespeare wrote *The Two Gentlemen of Verona*. Whereas some scholars believe that he had finished it by 1590, which would make it his very first play, others – the majority – think that it was completed in 1595 or, in other words, shortly after he had written *The Comedy of Errors* and *The Taming of the Shrew*. At all events, the relative simplicity of the characterisation and conventionality of the verse show that it was quite an early work. It was printed in the first collected edition of his plays, after his death, the First Folio of 1623. There are indications that the Folio text is a shortened version of a once longer play which was cut, perhaps to suit the limited resources of a small company of actors who had left London and were touring the country. It is certainly one of the shortest of Shakespeare's plays.

He took the main outlines of the plot from the story of Felix and Felismena, which forms an episode in a pastoral romance, the *Diana Enamorada*, written in Spanish by the Portuguese novelist and poet Jorge de Montemayor. This prose work was extremely popular. It was translated into French by Nicholas Colin in 1578 and into English by Bartholomew Yonge in 1582. Although Yonge's English translation was not published until 1598 (some years after *The Two Gentlemen* had been written), Shakespeare may have read it in manuscript or have picked up the story from another play based on the same episode, *The History of Felix and Philiomena*, the author of which is not known and the text of which has not survived, but which is recorded as having been performed at the court of Queen Elizabeth during the New Year festivities of 1585. This lost play might still have been in the repertory of the Lord Chamberlain's Men by the time Shakespeare had joined them and would thus have provided him with a readily available source for his own comedy. He may also have been influenced by 'The Wonderful History of Titus and Gisippus', a story told by Sir Thomas Elyot in a very different kind of work, his *Boke Named* the *Governour* (1531), a manual of advice on the education of young noblemen. Titus and Gisippus are two young men who find themselves in predicaments similar to those of Valentine and Proteus, and are praised by Elyot as ideal models of male friendship.

*The Two Gentlemen* has been one of Shakespeare's least popular plays in the theatre and, in fact, there is no record at all of its performance before December 1762, when it was presented by David Garrick at his Drury Lane Theatre. The comedy which Garrick directed, moreover, was not Shakespeare's original but an adaptation made by the Treasurer of the theatre, Benjamin Victor. Both versions were put on by John Philip Kemble, Shakespeare's at Drury Lane in 1790 and Victor's at Covent Garden in 1808. An operatic version with music composed by Henry Rowley Bishop had some success when it was staged at Covent Garden in 1821, but the three major attempts to revive an interest in Shakespeare's original comedy in the nineteenth century, by William Charles Macready, Charles Kean and Samuel Phelps, all failed. The production at the Court Theatre in 1904 was a remarkable one in that Harley Granville-Barker, one of the most adventurous directors of his time, not only produced it but also played the minor role of the servant, Speed. There was also a distinguished First Outlaw, Lewis Casson, who doubled the part with that of Sir Eglamour. *The Two Gentlemen* was put on in 1910 by William Poel's Elizabethan Stage Society and in 1925 at the Apollo Theatre under the direction of Robert Atkins, with John Gielgud as Valentine. One of the few successful productions in the play's history was by the Bristol Old Vic Company in 1951, of which the director was Dennis Carey with John Neville as Valentine. It has not been included frequently in the repertory at Stratford-on-Avon. Frank Benson staged it in 1910, Bridges-Adams in 1925 and Peter Hall in 1960 with Eric Porter as the Duke and Derek Godfrey as Proteus. The most recent Stratford production was in 1970, with Robin Philips directing, Ian Richardson as Valentine, Peter Egan as Proteus, Estelle Kohler as Silvia and Helen Mirren as Julia.

This production, directed by Don Taylor, was recorded at the BBC Television Centre in July 1983.

# INTRODUCTION TO
# THE TWO GENTLEMEN
# OF VERONA

## John Wilders

Whether or not *The Two Gentlemen of Verona* was Shakespeare's first play, it was certainly his first romantic comedy, and to that extent pointed in the direction he was to follow when he composed his great comedies such as *Much Ado About Nothing, As You Like It* and *Twelfth Night*. It is a 'romantic' play not only in the sense that it deals almost exclusively with the pains and pleasures of love, but because it is a dramatisation of one of those prose works known as romances of which the Elizabethans were extremely fond and which provided them with light, imaginative and gently instructive reading. The forefather of all the romances was the *Æthiopica* by the third-century Greek writer Heliodorus. This was circulated widely in manuscript, then in many printed editions, and was translated into all the major European languages. Under its influence a very large number of romances were composed in Renaissance Europe, including several which provided Shakespeare with the plots of his comedies, such as *Rosalynde* by Thomas Lodge (the source of *As You Like It*), *Pandosto* by Robert Greene (the source of *The Winter's Tale*), and the *Diana Enamorada* by the Portuguese writer Montemayor, from a version of which Shakespeare took the outlines of the plot of *The Two Gentlemen of Verona*.

Although the romance is a very flexible, infinitely expandable form, capable of accommodating every kind of material, all romances have some features in common. They are palpably works of fiction, abounding in unlikely coincidences and unrealistic conventions such as the disguise of women as men (and sometimes men as women) and consequent mistakes of identity. The action always takes place in no real geographical location but propels the characters into unfamiliar territory – as, in this play, Julia makes her solitary pilgrimage from Verona to Milan and Valentine, wandering in a strange forest, is chosen as their captain by a band of outlaws. The romances are usually made up of several inter-woven plots, each of which tends to break off at a point of suspense to be interrupted by a second plot which itself reaches a moment of crisis when it is broken by a third. Thus, in *The Two Gentlemen*, our attention is shifted between the affairs of Proteus at home and those of Valentine at the Emperor's court, and at the point when the latter is elected by the outlaws as their leader, we are brought back to the city to hear the serenade arranged by Proteus for Silvia. At the lowest level, the intertwining of different kinds of plot offers the reader the refreshment of variety and the mild excitement of suspense, and on a more sophisticated level it gives the author the opportunity to create parallels between plots and to set up contrasts, as when Proteus' infatuation with Julia is quickly followed by Valentine's for Silvia, or when Launce, the servant, reveals his love for a toothless dairymaid. The prose romances provided their readers with absorbing entertainment and, by the age of Elizabeth, with elaborate displays of literary artifice, richly ingenious metaphors, puns, quibbles and word-play which are also a feature of Shakespeare's comedies, including this one.

*The Two Gentlemen* contains several geographical inconsisten-cies. Valentine and Proteus both set off from Verona to Milan by sea, whereas Julia visualises making the journey by land. The Duke of Milan (who is also referred to as 'the Emperor') describes himself as living in Verona, and on his arrival in Milan Launce is greeted by his friend Speed with the words 'Welcome to Padua'. Such inconsistencies, probably the result of Shakespeare's over-sight, can actually help the audience to feel that they are in no place which can be located on a map but in a purely fictional country where no pressing political or domestic tasks trouble the characters, who are thereby left free to devote themselves to the overriding business of all romances, the processes of falling in and out of love, and all the embarrassments, confusions and dilemmas which they create. Sexual infatuation not only pushes forward the plot of *The Two Gentlemen* and occupies the minds of all the characters – so that even the Duke claims to have his eye on a lady – but is also the subject of practically all the dialogue. Love in this play is, variously, 'a grievous labour', 'a canker', 'a testy babe', 'an uncertain glory', 'a chameleon', 'a mighty lord', 'the soul's food', 'a figure trenched in ice', and 'a blinded god', depending on who happens to be possessed by it and whether or not his feelings are reciprocated. The subject of the play is the many forms in which love reveals itself, as friendship, loyalty, enslavement, infatuation, devotion, idealism, frustration and lust, and Shakespeare found in the conventions of romance, with its multiple narratives, its parallels and contrasts of plot and character, a form which was expansive enough to accommodate all these things.

In comparison with the characters of his later plays, the four main protagonists are not created with much depth or subtlety but they are the kind of people likely to be seized and perplexed by the changeable, violent emotions which are the dramatist's concern in this play. It is important to realise that both Proteus and Valentine are young and at a stage in their emotional and biological development which much interested Shakespeare, particularly at this point in his professional career. Having hitherto found love and intimacy with each other – with members of their own sex – each experiences for the first time the sudden shock of infatuation with a member of the opposite sex. In this they are like the young Romeo who, when we first see him, has just separated himself off from the gang of youths of his own age – Mercutio, Benvolio and the rest – and turned his affections towards the unattainable Rosaline; or like Claudio in *Much Ado About Nothing* who, before the play opens, has, as a soldier, known only the comradeship of his fellow-officers, but on his return from the front falls instantly in love with Hero; or like the poet of the *Sonnets* who is first enslaved by his adoration of a young man and later entangled in the charms of a dark lady. Proteus and Valentine are thus uncertain where their true loyalties lie, to each other or to their girl-friends, because each is caught in the process of changing from his adolescent into his mature self. To make matters more worrying, their affections seem to change as unpredictably as they themselves, and hence Valentine, hitherto immune to sexual attraction, becomes possessed by love for Silvia, and Proteus, formerly the devoted servant of Julia, becomes dazzled by Silvia from the moment he sees her:

Even as one heat another heat expels
Or as one nail by strength drives out another,
So the remembrance of my former love
Is by a newer object quite forgotten . . .
She is fair; and so is Julia that I love –
That I did love, for now my love is thaw'd;
Which like a waxen image 'gainst a fire
Bears no impression of the thing it was.

Proteus and Valentine, like the young men in *A Midsummer Night's Dream*, are unable to account for their sudden, unforeseen

changes of affection. Although they are not fully realised characters, they do behave consistently with their age, and also with their
sex: it is the men who are giddy and undependable; the women,
having matured earlier, remain steadily faithful to their first loves
throughout. First and foremost the play portrays the attempts of
two young men to discover who they are, attempts made more
difficult by the fact that they are emotionally unstable. Valentine,
who originally scoffs at the love-lorn Proteus, no sooner arrives in
Milan than he finds himself infatuated. He has become a different
kind of person, 'metamorphosed with a mistress', as his servant
Speed describes him, 'that, when I look on you, I can hardly think
you my master'. Valentine himself describes his transformation
more eloquently:

Ay, Proteus, but that life is alter'd now;
I have done penance for contemning Love,
Whose high imperious thoughts have punish'd me
With bitter fasts, with penitential groans,
With nightly tears, and daily heart-sore sighs;
For, in revenge of my contempt of love,
Love hath chas'd sleep from my enthralled eyes
And made them watchers of mine own heart's sorrow.
O gentle Proteus, Love's a mighty lord,
And hath so humbled me as I confess
There is no woe to his correction,
Nor to his service no such joy on earth.

They may not know who they are, but they do know that the
strange feelings which possess them admit of no resistance.

*The Two Gentlemen of Verona* is a romance and it is also a debate
– or rather a series of debates – on travel and education, on loyalty
to friends and parents, but mostly, again, on the absorbing and
paradoxical sensations of love. The first debate occurs at the very
opening of the play in which Valentine argues for the benefits of
foreign travel and Proteus for the necessity of remaining at home
with his mistress, and, like typical debaters, each supports his case
by quoting written authorities. According to Proteus, to be in love
is a sign of a refined sensibility:

Yet writers say, as in the sweetest bud
The eating canker dwells, so eating love
Inhabits in the finest wits of all.

According to Valentine, on the other hand, love is a sign of
premature decay:

And writers say, as the most forward bud
Is eaten by the canker ere it blow,
Even so by love the young and tender wit
Is turn'd to folly, blasting in the bud,
Losing his verdure even in the prime,
And all the fair effects of future hopes.

In the little soliloquy with which Proteus ends the discussion, he neatly defines their opposing points of view:

He after honour hunts, I after love;
He leaves his friends to dignify them more:
I leave myself, my friends, and all for love.

As with most of the debates in this very argumentative play, their differences are not resolved, probably because Shakespeare recognised that love could be at the same time ennobling and degrading, depending on whether you happen to be in love or not. Each of the young men, the one eager for fresh experiences, the other captivated by present ones, sticks to his point of view as they take their leave. Speed, who appears at the end of the same scene, also has his point of view: he is not interested in love but only in money.

The conversation between Julia and her maid Lucetta in the next scene also takes the form of a debate, this time on the merits of Proteus, in which Lucetta defends him and Julia, hiding her real feelings, argues against him:

*Jul.* And wouldst thou have me cast my love on him?
*Luc.* Ay, if you thought your love not cast away.
*Jul.* Why, he, of all the rest, hath never mov'd me.
*Luc.* Yet he, of all the rest, I think, best loves ye.
*Jul.* His little speaking shows his love but small.
*Luc.* Fire that's closest kept burns most of all.
*Jul.* They do not love that do not show their love.
*Luc.* O, they love least that let men know their love.

This is a kind of formal argument, made more apparent by the way in which one line chimes in with another, but the motives which lie behind it are not unsubtle: whereas the waiting maid speaks up for Proteus in order to induce her mistress to a confession of love, the mistress pretends to despise him in order to conceal her real feelings. The truth is that Julia is in some confusion, unable to resist her love for Proteus, yet anxious to keep up the appearance of self-control proper to a young lady. Hence she tears up Proteus' letter while Lucetta is with her, but pieces it together again when

she is left alone. She expresses these conflicting impulses in a
soliloquy which is really a little debate with herself:

> Fie, fie, how wayward is this foolish love,
> That like a testy babe will scratch the nurse,
> And presently, all humbled, kiss the rod!
> How churlishly I chid Lucetta hence,
> When willingly I would have had her here!
> How angerly I taught my brow to frown,
> When inward joy enforc'd my heart to smile!

Like Proteus and Valentine later in the play, Julia finds herself
caught between two equally demanding claims or obligations,
those of love and modesty, and she is unable to shake off either of
them. She manages to get the best of both worlds by allowing her
maid to pick the letter up for her. Proteus, in the following scene,
is in an almost identical situation, trying to conceal Silvia's letter
from his father. Both are going through the struggles and embarrassments of growing up, trying to work out their relationships
with other people and themselves.

The really big inward debates take place, however, in the mind
of Proteus, whose already divided character becomes enmeshed in
further emotional complications. Having been forced by his father
to abandon Julia and join Valentine in Milan, he not only finds that
his friend is now head over heels in love, but, himself, becomes
infatuated with Sylvia, the mistress of his closest companion. Like
Julia earlier in the play, Proteus finds himself on the horns of a
dilemma, divided between his vows to Julia and his loyalty to
Valentine on the one hand, and his passion for Silvia on the other.
He obviously cannot remain faithful to all three of them and
whatever he decides must inevitably amount to a betrayal. The
nature of his quandary could not be more precisely stated:

> To leave my Julia, shall I be forsworn;
> To love fair Silvia, shall I be forsworn;
> To wrong my friend, I shall be much forsworn;
> And ev'n that pow'r which gave me first my oath
> Provokes me to this threefold perjury:
> Love bade me swear, and Love bids me forswear.
> O sweet-suggesting Love, if thou hast sinn'd,
> Teach me, thy tempted subject, to excuse it!
> At first I did adore a twinkling star,
> But now I worship a celestial sun . . .
> I cannot leave to love, and yet I do;

But there I leave to love where I should love.
Julia I lose, and Valentine I lose;
If I keep them, I needs must lose myself;
If I lose them, thus find I by their loss:
For Valentine, myself; for Julia, Silvia.

The speech is composed of paradoxes and contradictions because Proteus finds that he is, himself, paradoxical, caught between contradictions, urged on by impulses which he both embraces and despises. Like Valentine he is a changed man, but unlike Valentine he is torn between the pledges made by his former self and the desires his present self is unable to resist. The one idea to which Shakespeare keeps returning in this play is the essentially divided nature of these young men, caught between their loves and loyalties to other people and themselves. It has been pointed out that the play tends to fall into passages of duologue, soliloquies and asides, and therefore does not have the variety and expansiveness of Shakespeare's later work. Once its basic form has been perceived, however, the reason behind this simple construction becomes clear. It consists of a series of discussions between opposing points of view or between opposing elements within a single character.

This kind of conflict reaches its greatest complexity in the episode where Proteus provides the serenade outside Silvia's window. Before the lady herself appears four characters are present: Thurio, Proteus, the disguised Julia and the Host. Each of them interprets the performance in a different way. Thurio believes that the music has been arranged in order that Silvia may be induced to look favourably on him; Proteus, on the other hand, knows that he is using the serenade to win Silvia for himself; Julia, disguised as a boy, is desolated by her lover's unfaithfulness; and the Host, who has no personal interest at all in the affair, just listens to the music and then falls fast asleep. Each character is living within his own subjective world, and this becomes clear when Julia and the Host converse with each other:

*Host.* How do you, man? The music likes you not.
*Julia.* You mistake; the musician likes me not.
*Host.* Why, my pretty youth?
*Julia.* He plays false, father.
*Host.* How, out of tune on the strings?
*Julia.* Not so; but yet so false that he grieves my very heart-strings.

The threads can be unravelled only when all the characters know the truth and all the conflicting points of view have become reconciled.

The two servants, Launce and Speed, provide earthy comic relief, but Launce, the more fully-developed of the two, finds himself placed in situations comparable to those of his superiors. As soon as we have seen Proteus take his leave of Julia we are given Launce's account of the parting between his parents and himself with his dog, Crab. The two episodes have a number of details in common, so that the latter serves as a kind of parody of the former. In the first episode Julia is practically silent, expressing the speechlessness of true devotion, whereas Proteus is extravagantly eloquent:

> Here is my hand for my true constancy;
> And when that hour o'erslips me in the day
> Wherein I sigh not, Julia, for thy sake,
> The next ensuing hour some foul mischance
> Torment me for my love's forgetfulness!
> My father stays my coming; answer not;
> The tide is now – nay, not thy tide of tears:
> That tide will stay me longer than I should.

Launce and Crab, too, have just come from a leavetaking but, although the whole family have given way without inhibition to their grief, the dog, naturally, has, like Julia, remained silent:

> My mother weeping, my father wailing, my sister crying, our maid howling, our cat wringing her hands, and all our house in a great perplexity; yet did not this cruel-hearted cur shed one tear. He is a stone, a very pebble stone, and has no more pity in him than a dog.

The moment of parting, which in the previous episode had been full of pathos, now appears simply farcical, and the speechlessness which, in Julia, was evidence of devotion, in Crab is a sign of heartlessness. Both dog and master, each in his different way, provide a comic contrast to the young lovers. Launce's exaggerated displays of emotion are absurd counterparts to the heightened, all-consuming passions which possess the young gentlefolk, and Crab's silent acceptance of all situations makes the eloquence of the human characters seem exaggerated. The dog's lack of concern for other people (it is he who makes water against a gentlewoman's farthingale) is a necessarily silent but nonetheless pointed criticism of the tendency of all the other characters to become entangled in one another. Crab's self-love, as Launce interprets it, adds another colour to the spectrum of love which Shakespeare creates in the play as a whole. Even he has his own unique point of view.

The tension between conflicting attitudes becomes most acute, as we might expect, in the final scene, the moment which has provoked the strongest protests from Shakespeare's critics. By now Shakespeare has written himself into a situation which admits of no really satisfactory outcome. Proteus, in his banishment, has been forcibly separated from Silvia; Silvia has taken flight, pursued by the loathsome Proteus; Julia, devotedly following him, witnesses her lover's attempt to commit a rape on Silvia; and, when Valentine intervenes, the characters begin to see the true state of things for the first time. At last perceiving his friend's treachery, Valentine is immediately thrust into an impossible dilemma of a kind which, by now, has become typical of the play. He is divided between his love for Silvia, which requires that he should avenge himself on Proteus, and his friendship for Proteus which demands that he should refrain. Like his friend, at an earlier point in the play, he is forced to choose between the claims of love and those of friendship. Unlike Proteus, however, he decides in favour of friendship, but only when the former has shown his contrition:

> Then I am paid;
> And once again I do receive thee honest.
> Who by repentance is not satisfied
> Is nor of heaven nor of earth, for these are pleas'd;
> By penitence th'Eternal's wrath's appeas'd.

His reference to Christian doctrine ('forgive us our trespasses as we should forgive them that trespass against us') suggests that Shakespeare intends us to take his decision seriously, and, though he is nobly denying himself the woman he adores, we might be able to approve his choice were it not that he goes on to demonstrate his loyalty by spontaneously handing Silvia over to his rival:

> And, that my love may appear plain and free,
> All that was mine in Silvia I give thee.

Such unhesitating altruism is consistent with what we have seen of Valentine. He has, throughout, been the trusting innocent, remaining loyal to one woman, unaware of the treachery practised on him by his friend. But such high-mindedness, hard to accept even from a simple idealist like Valentine, shows no concern for poor Silvia who finds herself thrown into the arms of a man she despises, nor (did he only know it) for Julia who sees the man she loves handed over to another woman. 'There are by this time', as Quiller-Couch tartly commented, 'no gentlemen in Verona.' In resolving one problem, Valentine has created two others and it is a situation which, in real life, would be intolerable. Fortunately, however, we are not in real life but in an imaginary forest outside a non-existent Milan or Padua or Verona, and in this romance-setting Julia performs the conventional romance gesture: she reveals her true identity, instantly regains her lover's affection, and releases Silvia (who, understandably, says not a word throughout these proceedings) to rejoin Valentine. Shakespeare has solved his impossible problem but at the expense of credibility. It is the kind of satisfactory ending which makes us realise the improbability of such resolutions in the world we actually live in.

The Two Gentlemen of Verona shows Shakespeare making experiments with situations he was to develop more subtly later in his career. The disguised Julia is the prototype of the disguised Portia, Rosalind and Viola; the friendship of the young men is a sketch for the similar relationship between Antonio and Bassanio; the shifts of affection were to develop into the more complicated cross-wooings of A Midsummer Night's Dream; the move from the court to the country, already a feature of the prose romances well before this play was written, reappears in The Dream, As You Like It, Cymbeline, The Winter's Tale, and even in King Lear; the use of the comic sub-plot to parallel and cast light on the main plot becomes a feature of all Shakespeare's comedies which, like this one, display the delights and absurdities of love in all its manifestations. It is because these features were later developed in dramatically more accomplished plays that The Two Gentlemen has been neglected or regarded condescendingly by both criticis and theatre audiences. Yet the sketchbook of a great artist is of interest not simply as a series of trials for more major works. It has its own inherent value. Shakespeare plots the developing complexities of his narrative with great skill; the verse, often scarcely distinguishable from that of a dozen Elizabethan love poets, can take on an astonishing lyrical intensity and, in spite of the conventional mode in which the play was conceived, it does deal, at the same time ironically and with sympathy, with a perennial experience, the search of necessarily unstable individuals for some lasting, stable identity.

# THE PRODUCTION

## Henry Fenwick

Shaun Sutton, producer of the Shakespeare cycle for the BBC, has
known writer/director Don Taylor 'for some years as a colleague',
he says. 'But I'd never worked with him in any producer/director
mode. Then one day Keith Williams, the head of our department,
said, "Did you know it was the dream of Don Taylor's life ever
since he was at Oxford to direct *The Two Gentlemen of Verona*?
He's studied it and he's passionate!"' It is not the dream of many
directors' lives to direct *Two Gentlemen* – it is not one of
Shakespeare's most popular plays – and Sutton was at that time
actually pondering whom he should get to direct the piece. 'You
can't be fed a more direct cue than that,' Sutton laughs, 'so the
next time I met Don I said, "Will you come and do *The Two
Gentlemen of Verona*?" and his face blossomed and he said, "Of
course I will!" It's a very happy conclusion. Don's a terrific
director and he pointed out and underlined things in this play that
might not have occurred to a man less obsessed.'

'I wanted to do the play for two reasons,' Taylor explains. 'One,
I was taught by a very remarkable man at Oxford who had a
particular passion for this play – his name was Robert Browning –
and he made me attend to the play for the first time. Like
everybody else I tended to dismiss it. We had a couple of long
sessions on it, just saying look what it's about, read it carefully, see
what issues are being raised in this play and how important they
are. The other thing – I was in Boston four years ago and I saw
what I'm sure was the worst-acted production I've ever seen in my
life, a student production of *The Two Gentlemen of Verona*. The
acting was of an unbelievable dreadfulness, they had no technique,
but they loved the play, they understood the speed it should go and
they understood what it was about, so it was a wonderful evening
in the theatre. You very quickly in the first quarter of an hour
adjust to the actual level of technical achievement that is facing you
– that's why you can enjoy a school production of Shakespeare –
then, as always happens with Shakespeare, the play begins to

perform its usual magic. It's a real charmer of a play when it works. I made a mental note, reminding myself that I would love to do the play.

'A lot of people are very rude about it,' he acknowledges, 'including most of the academics. This play gets all kinds of rubbishing from critics who assert that there are great chunks missing, it's two or three plays put together, and that Shakespeare was very careless and there are lots of inconsistencies. All of which may be true. Nobody knows anything about the provenance of the play and there are one or two extraordinary clangers, which we've had to change slightly in order to make dramatic sense. For example, the characters get confused about where they are. When it's quite clear that they've all gone to Milan the Duke says, "There is a lady in Verona here . . ." They cannot *possibly* be in Verona under any circumstances! It's a mistake of some kind. So we've changed the line to ". . . in the city here". Similarly, at one point when Proteus' servant, Launce, has followed his master to Milan Valentine's page Speed welcomes him by saying, "Welcome to Padua". Now that might have been a joke – this is Will Kemp and his sidekick on stage and if you were to have Morecambe and Wise's scripts in front of you, just the words, you would find it quite hard, particularly at a gap of 300 years, to work out what they actually *did*. And it's what they do that makes you laugh, it's not the words. There's not the slightest doubt that Will Kemp, who played Launce, was a great creative comedian, and when Speed says "Welcome to Padua" you've only got to imagine the kind of double take that Eric Morecambe might do! So it may well be that that is exactly what they said. Or it might be a silly mistake. In fact we changed that – we tried to make a joke of it but we couldn't find the gag, so we changed it to "Welcome to the court". But apart from these little oddments, as a dramatic structure the play works marvellously well, in the sense that each scene tells you what you want to know next. It's a marvellously put together piece of work – it may be accident, it may be a mess of half a dozen plays, but it works like a dream when you're actually putting it together.'

Taylor is anxious not to put his case for the play too emphatically. 'One must be sensible about this – it's the first of that great line of romantic comedies that's going to produce *Twelfth Night, As You Like It* and *A Midsummer Night's Dream*, and it's not as good a play as those, you wouldn't expect it to be, it's his first try. In a sense it's a compendium of all those later plays: it's got lots of scenes in it which foreshadow later scenes, which are greater scenes, most of them. But if Shakespeare had died at thirty, as lots of people did in those days, it would be one of the greatest comedies in English because we wouldn't have all his others.'

*The Two Gentlemen* has never been a play with a large following. Its conventional plot of faithless lover, friend betrayed, girl disguised as boy, has a great deal of charm but also a lot of artificiality. And there are obvious difficulties in producing the play for a mass television audience. 'There are certain things in the first half an hour of *The Two Gentlemen of Verona*,' admits Taylor, 'which are very much to do with Elizabethan fashion, and unless you present them very carefully to a modern audience they are not going to know what's going on. The approach to the play for television was to recognise that there are elements in it which are fairly alien, not to try to explain that, because you can't explain it to them. You've got to face up to that. This play quite clearly comes out of that maniacal fashion for everything Italian that swept over England in the 1580s. For example: the first book of Italian madrigals to be printed in English was published in 1588. *Musica Transalpina* it was called, and it contained fifty-seven madrigals by people like Marenzio and Ferrabosco—he actually lived in London for a while. This book had been circulating in manuscript for ten years, and had been instrumental in helping to unleash the whole English madrigal school which flourished for the next fifty years. Some of the English composers, particularly Dowland, were quite as good as their Italian contemporaries, and of course the poets were very much better, but they were all swept away, delighted by everything Italian—Italian poetry, Italian music, Italian behaviour, Italian manners, Italian history, Castiglione, *The Courtier*, the ideal Renaissance gentleman, all that. Cheap Italian novelle came over in their shiploads to be translated, to provide cheap, thrilling Italian stories for people who had no idea, probably, where Italy was, just knowing that it was where it was all at! This enormous fashion swept over the arts in England and over educated men in England; English poetry was totally obsessed with the need to imitate, to "overgo" was the word they used, the best Italian models: Spenser, all the English sonneteers – half of those Elizabethan sonnets were translations from Petrarch or from French poets who had translated the same original source. They thought the English language was rough and uncultured and heavy and that the Italian language was sweet and melodious and beautiful, and that the poet's job was to try to produce in our barbaric rough Northern tongue the sweetness and music of Italian poetry. That's what they all thought they were doing. And when you look back to the poetry that was being written at the beginning of the century it *was* rough and crude and uncultured by comparison.

'This play comes entirely out of this fashion for a fantasised Italian Renaissance. The real Italian Renaissance was ever so nasty, a blood-stained and violent business, but there was this beautiful fantasy world and arty dream, in which these stories took place. Most of Shakespeare's plots are taken from Italian sources, Italian tales brought over for the consumption of the beginning of the English book market. So Shakespeare, or the people who ran his theatre, decided it would be a good thing. Like all theatrical entrepreneurs, they were thinking, "We must try to hit this fashion", so Shakespeare writes them a play which is utterly conventional in that sense, it appeals absolutely to the fashion of the times.'

Very little is known about the play's stage history before the mid-eighteenth century. 'I'm not absolutely sure the play was meant for the public theatre,' says Taylor, 'because it's extremely sophisticated in a lot of ways. There are whole series of cross-references – so many that it can't be accidental – to Marlowe's poem, *Hero and Leander*, which came out just before Marlowe's death and caused a sensation, this overtly homosexual poem written in the most lucid and glowing ornamental tones. In the first scene the two educated young men, Valentine and Proteus, two young students is what they really are, joke together:

Pro.   Upon some book I love, I'll pray for thee.
Val.   That's on some shallow story of deep love:
      How young Leander cross'd the Hellespont.
Pro.   That's a deep story, of a deeper love;
      For he was more than over shoes in love.

That's the first of the references and there are eight or nine of them in the play. It's clear it's referring to what among educated circles was the current sensation, the way everyone talks about Salman Rushdie now, this extraordinary talent that's burst upon the world. Marlowe's *Hero and Leander* was what everyone was talking about: Shakespeare was obviously interested, fascinated I would imagine, by what the poem taught him, keeps on referring to it all the way through. And there are also long passages in the play which are simply parody, send-ups of current styles. For example, when Proteus is telling Silvia's suitor, Thurio, how he must write poems to her, he comes out with an extraordinary list of the current clichés of Elizabethan verse.

'It's a play which has got one eye on a sophisticated audience which knows about these things, and against that it's got Will Kemp in it. But suppose it was written for the Inns of Court, as *Love's Labour's Lost* probably was, i.e. for an audience of educated young men, people like Proteus and Valentine. It's not out of the question that they would enjoy Will Kemp, as a lot of intellectuals love Morecambe and Wise. In a sense Will Kemp is dragged into this play: Launce's bits are almost like individual stand-up comic routines – he comes on to do his number and goes off – except that being Shakespeare he links each bit with the theme of the play. There's that wonderful moment when after the lovers have all been getting into terrible messes Launce comes on and does a parody soliloquy about how he fell in love with this awful milkmaid, which sends up everything the others have just done. You get the same with his first speech when Julia and Proteus have just said a tearful farewell, then Launce comes on crying his eyes out. I don't think that puts out of court the thought that it maybe was written for the young men rather than for the public theatre. It wasn't a play that was very popular in the public theatre – the most popular play in Shakespeare's lifetime was *Titus Andronicus*, they loved all that, the hands chopped off, the gore, like nowadays if you're in trouble you put on *Dracula* or something like that. That means you have certain problems in presenting it for a mass audience.'

As producer Shaun Sutton sanguinely says, however, 'I don't see why it shouldn't appeal to a large audience. After all, it is about teenagers and their emotions. Their behaviour and reactions are impulsive and teenage. Their jokes and awful puns are teenage. Above all, their love is teenage. They fall in love instantly and just as quickly fall out again, not hesitating to betray a comrade in the process, on the excuse that all is fair in love. The fact that they are in graceful dresses rather than jeans doesn't matter, they're the same sort of people inside.'

Casting the lovers of *The Two Gentlemen* very young was, Taylor says, one of his first decisions. 'I would like them all to have been seventeen really, but the way the English profession is organised that's not possible. These are about as young as the profession could provide. Tessa Peake-Jones has been in a couple of my wife [Ellen Dryden]'s plays and I've known her work for a long time. The others were found by exhaustive auditions and by ringing up the drama schools saying, "Who have you just got rid of? What are your latest crop like?" The play has to do with the immense confusion that love causes; one of the biggest themes in Shakespeare is why do people fall in love with the wrong people? For a man who had a wife and kids at home and was involved in all kinds of other relationships in London it was always close to his heart. Very young people fall in love and don't know how to cope and make all the ABC mistakes. Because that is very funny a lot of the play is funny, but then it changes and becomes almost anarchic. Proteus knows he's wrong right from the start but he's totally obsessed by his desire for this girl. The thing that Tyler [Butterworth] brings to the role is charm. You think, "Oh, the poor silly boy, look what he's doing now", whereas if it were cast round about twenty-five or thirty it would get a very nasty taste – you would think, "This chap ought to know better!"'

The first thing Taylor told costume designer Dinah Collin, she recalls, was that it was an adolescent play and that it must be set earlier than Elizabethan. They settled on a Renaissance setting: 'There was an absolutely massive Renaissance drawings exhibition at the British Museum,' she remembers, 'and it was one of the most exciting things I've ever seen. The way the figures moved and the clothes didn't seem to get in the way seemed to be exactly what he wanted.' One picture she used as inspiration was, she says, of 'youths falling over one another – it was very much about the physical side rather than clothes imposing big shapes. And I thought the women ought to have the same quality: you were aware of skin! The Flora of Botticelli which I used for Joanne Pearce as Silvia seemed perfect for this look. I wanted to make things as near as possible to the way modern clothes work, where you just put one garment on top of another, but of course it is just not possible! The girl who made Cloten's very elaborate costumes for *Cymbeline* is absolutely wonderful at working out how to make a material work and she made a pair of tights for me that fit like a pair of jeans but still had a period feel to them.'

Taylor is anxious not to stress the significance of the visual element unduly: 'I don't think it matters what they wear on the whole. I have seen wonderful performances of Shakespeare played in rehearsal rooms. What matters is that you attend to the poetry, what matters is that you attend to the actual fabric of the play, and as long as you do that you can't destroy them. If you start worrying about design or costume or what it looks like or pictures that's the wrong way round and the results will be disaster. I think I'm the only practising writer who has directed one of these plays [he is the author of, among other plays, *Paradise Restored*, *In Hiding*, and the soon-to-be-screened *The Testament of John*], so I start from a slightly different position: I want to do this because it's great poetry and great drama, not because of what I can make it look like. The fact that this production at times looks like certain paintings is something that grew out of the production, in no way started it. I have no interest in trying to imitate great painters; the fact that one or two shots look like Botticelli or whoever is simply because I gave the designers certain briefs about style of scenery and style of costume, and then I put frames round them in certain ways. One tends to come to the same kind of conclusion as the great painters simply because one's eyes are trained by these people. But I didn't have the slightest intention of trying to imitate painters. I think that's an irrelevant thing to do.'

One of the major problems in designing the play was linked directly to the problem of presenting the play to a mass audience. The essentially literary nature of much of the dialogue, the verbal rallying, the battles of wit, pose a problem of comprehension. 'In order to make that a little clearer,' Taylor says, 'I made a design decision which is nowhere in the play. In order to illuminate the play I put the thing into its tradition by creating a kind of Garden of Courtly Love for the lovers to disport themselves. I made it as artificial and created as possible, as though it's something arranged by the duke in which the young people can amuse themselves in the fashionable manner. There are poets all over the place and there are lutenists everywhere and there are gilded cupids – who are actually a couple of Milan kids employed to litter the place with conventional images, so I have them seen as ordinary kids at the end sweeping up, while the lutenists repair their lutes. A Renaissance Disneyland. That was a directorial decision I might not make on the stage but I thought it would help to get over to the audience the artificial nature of all this – an elegant literary game.

'What I asked the designer to do was something which is very very difficult indeed – to create a degree of elegant stylisation which would not be as strongly expressionistic as you might do on the stage, because that alienates television audiences. Television is largely a naturalistic medium because of what other people do with it; television viewers like to know where they are and what they're doing. But to put *Two Gentlemen* in real streets and a real forest only does a disservice to the play, particularly to the final scene in the forest, which is really the exploration of a series of poetic images and has nothing to do with real forests at all. A forest in Shakespeare is always a place where people go to find the truth. And you can't take the outlaws seriously: you can't do them as dangerous, frightening men. They're the Red Shadow and his gang from *Desert Song*: "We're all gentlemen, you know!" There is even a reference to Robin Hood: "By the bare scalp of Robin Hood's fat friar", which is a wink to the audience. I asked Barbara [Gosnold, the set designer] to give me patterned floors everywhere and an arrangement of arches and columns: a dream of the Italian Renaissance, all open and interrelated and beautiful to look at. I wanted that blue sky! I'm very pleased with the result and the costumes match it very well. There are times when Silvia looks like Flora in the *Primavera* when she comes in – but that's a case of using the artist's vision because it seems to have something relevant to say about this play.'

Barbara Gosnold and her assistant, Barry Read, worked out an arrangement of towers and arches that call on both Botticelli and Fra Angelico, 'fairly artificial but flowery and with a fresh spring feel,' Barbara Gosnold says she wanted. The towers – one a little golden cage for Silvia, the other for Julia – 'I wanted to be like a little dovecote, very romantic and beautiful,' she explains. The arrangement of arches sometimes results in pictures that look like triptychs, while the most difficult locale to stylise, the forest, was also based on a Botticelli painting, with bare trunks stabbing towards the sky from a green-carpeted floor.

An extra pressure on the design was Taylor's preferred way of working. 'I tend to differ from most of my colleagues in that I am a very fervent advocate of continuous performance – most of this was done in great long chunks, twenty-minute chunks. I think that the film-making approach to television is ludicrous, it's a waste of the resources. If you want to make a film, go make a film. You can do other things in a television studio – you can get that dangerous element of performance. There were at least two occasions in this play where an actress did things in the heat of performance that were far beyond anything she'd reached in rehearsal: insights and perceptions that only performance can achieve. It seems to me far more important in a play that was designed for the theatre to go for that rather than for very carefully arranged pictures and very carefully angled lighting; which is what you get when you do it shot by shot. You destroy the actors' performances when you do that. English actors are very good at *imitating* performances, they have been trained to, so they will do the line exactly the same in intonation and exactly the same in speed as you told them to do it and as they would have done it in a complete run, but it will have no life in it, no imaginative fire. I would like to have done the whole play straight through in one take, and I have done on previous productions [his BBC TV *The Crucible*]. I broke this play more than I've broken up any in a long time, but I did each scene complete and, in the case of the third act, I did about four scenes run together so we had about twenty minutes of continuous acting. At no point did I stop any scene to get a better angle and I don't think it looks any worse, I don't think the lighting looks crude – Sam [Barclay] did a marvellous job. You need a lighting man who will realise we are accepting certain compromises here, we know that we can't do it exactly as we would do it if we were doing it shot by shot. It's the lighting man who suffers most.'

Another major decision in dictating the style of the performance was Taylor's resolution to use authentic music, researched and edited by Anthony Rooley. 'You take a great risk,' he says, 'if you don't use the music of the age. It was the greatest age of English music, except perhaps for Purcell; in Dowland we had a very great composer, and in Morley and the rest we had very good composers. In a lot of cases of Shakespeare's plays the music for the play survives, but nothing survives for this. Everyone knows Schubert's setting for "Who is Silvia?", which is quite alien – a nineteenth-century art song. One of the earliest decisions I made, because it is basically an entertainment play with deeper levels, was that I would use a *lot* of music in it, contemporary music, and that I would put it into the hands of the experts. There's been an enormous growth industry in the last fifteen years of authentic music, music which is properly researched. I'd heard a lot of records of Anthony and the Consort of Music – Elizabethan experts. Tony had just completed a series on Radio 3 called *The English Madrigal*, music from 1588 to 1630, and I thought I would like to bring him in as a colleague and he's been with it from the start. He found the music that we used for "Silvia", which is a very famous piece by Robert Johnson for another song – originally a setting for Ben Jonson's poem, "Have you seen but a bright lily grow", slightly changed because the verse pattern is slightly different.' In fact, as Taylor points out, Shakespeare has written the dialogue in the scene of the serenading of Silvia to fit the time a pavane and galliard would take. 'When you work it out, the bit of dialogue from the beginning of the music until the text says it changes is about the kind of length you'd expect a pavane to take, and the next stretch of dialogue is the length of a galliard – which is the combination you would expect musicians to play in those circumstances, slow and stately then lively and joyful. When we rehearsed it we were within a few seconds and just had to adjust the speed slightly.

'The sound of the original instruments is so beautiful – we used a beautiful thing called an orpharion, which is basically a little guitar but strung with metal strings so it creates a tinkling, icy, glittering sound. It seems to me that the sound of that music and the harmony of the music of that period is of a piece with Shakespeare's own word music, it's a product of the same culture, and I think you take great risks if you move out of that. If you do the tragedies it's quite reasonable to commission original scores, I think, but you are moving into a different culture and have to be aware of that. Dowland, Morley, all the great composers, are of exactly the same historical moment as Shakespeare and the sound is right. We used one Italian piece to give the audience an indication of what I'm doing: the play starts with a madrigal in Italian saying "Oh, what a wonderful thing is youth", and it also covers the credits at the end, so the play is topped and tailed with an Italian madrigal to show we are making a gesture to the fashion for everything Italian. Also I staged a lot of it live – conventional wisdom says you mime to playback and put it together afterwards, but it's not the same when you mime to playback, you don't get the same feeling. The first time the orpharion player came into outside rehearsal it changed the actors' performances, without question. It intensified and deepened them. It's true that it means you're running great risks because it's all got to be right, we couldn't fiddle about with it afterwards. But there's too much fiddling about in television anyway.'

If any part of *The Two Gentlemen of Verona* has caused problems with the critics it is its final scene, where love confusions are resolved in a few lines, where Valentine in an outburst of forgiveness and friendship offers Silvia to Proteus, where all problems and conflicts are made up, as it were, by a wave of the wand. 'The academics say all kinds of silly things – too short, no motivation. We live in a post-naturalist, post-Chekhov age where if someone is going to change his mind you expect to see it for the previous ten pages, gradually happening. But the thing that Robert Browning gave me was – he said, "Take a look at the last scene, at what's actually said." The criticisms don't matter – it's *poetry* we're dealing with. It's a marvellous piece of compressed poetry which says a great deal in a very short space. Valentine has a wonderful speech that could come straight out of *Hamlet*:

Thou common friend, that's without faith or love –
For such is a friend now; treacherous man,
Thou hast beguil'd my hopes; nought but mine eye
Could have persuaded me. Now I dare not say
I have one friend alive: thou wouldst disprove me.
Who should be trusted, when one's own right hand
Is perjured to the bosom? Proteus,
I am sorry I must never trust thee more,
But count the world a stranger for thy sake.

'The scene brings up huge moral issues: how do we behave with each other? As for Proteus' repentance, although it seems sudden, it's not sudden when you look at the rest of the performance: all the time he's known he was wrong, right from the first soliloquy he's been living in a kind of self-induced fantasy. As soon as he's confronted with reality it all collapses at once. It's not in any way an easy ending to the play; it only takes five lines, but that's because Shakespeare is a great poet, not because he's incompetent! Proteus says:

            were man
But constant, he were perfect. That one error
Fills him with faults . . .

That creates all drama: we're not constant, we're not perfect. This is what Robert Browning gave me when I was twenty. You have to examine each word, as you must with poetry. It's bottomless. Looking at it again, I can see there are still subtle implications we missed. Well, they are there for the next time!'

# THE BBC TV CAST AND
# PRODUCTION TEAM

The cast for the BBC Television production was as follows:

| | |
|---|---|
| DUKE OF MILAN | Paul Daneman |
| VALENTINE | John Hudson |
| PROTEUS | Tyler Butterworth |
| ANTONIO | Michael Byrne |
| THURIO | David Collings |
| SIR EGLAMOUR | Frank Barrie |
| SPEED | Nicholas Kaby |
| LAUNCE | Tony Haygarth |
| PANTHINO | John Woodnutt |
| HOST | Michael Graham Cox |
| JULIA | Tessa Peake-Jones |
| SILVIA | Joanne Pearce |
| LUCETTA | Hetta Charnley |
| SERVANT | Daniel Flynn |
| FIRST OUTLAW | Adam Kurakin |
| SECOND OUTLAW | John Baxter |
| THIRD OUTLAW | Andrew Burt |
| CUPIDS | Charlotte Richardson |
| | Jonathan Taylor |
| LUTENISTS | Bill Badley |
| | Tom Finucane |
| | Robin Jeffrey |
| CRAB | Bella |
| | |
| PRODUCTION MANAGER | Brian Morgan |
| DIRECTOR'S ASSISTANT | Patricia Harrington |
| PRODUCTION ASSOCIATE | Fraser Lowden |
| MUSIC RESEARCH | Anthony Rooley |
| LITERARY CONSULTANT | John Wilders |
| MAKE-UP ARTIST | Elizabeth Moss |
| COSTUME DESIGNER | Dinah Collin |

| | |
|---|---|
| SOUND | Ray Angel |
| LIGHTING | Sam Barclay |
| DESIGNER | Barbara Gosnold |
| SCRIPT EDITOR | David Snodin |
| PRODUCER | Shaun Sutton |
| DIRECTOR | Don Taylor |

The production was recorded between 25 and 31 July 1983.

# THE TEXT

## Don Taylor

The biggest problem for a director in presenting *The Two Gentlemen of Verona* for a mass medium is not in the structural inconsistencies some academics see in the play, which are more apparent than real, but in the fact that the play bears all the signs of having been written to hit a contemporary fashion, or series of fashions, and that these fashions are now long dead, known only to literary historians. The play's deep and powerful examination of the inconsistencies and consequences of love among very young people, and the high quality of much of its lyric verse, makes it indispensable, the first of the great line of anti-romantic comedies with which Shakespeare was to enrich us. Heavy cutting is the philistine solution, and unbalances the structure of the play, so the problem of fashion has to be faced square on.

The most overwhelming of all these fashionable elements, and the one which, in a sense, embraces all the rest, is the mania for everything Italian that dominated English culture in the 1580s and 1590s. The influence was widespread over the whole field of culture, where Machiavelli, Castiglione, Tasso and Ariosto struggled for dominance in the thought of educated Englishmen. The ideal of the Renaissance gentleman particularly, the young man who is soldier, scholar, diplomat, poet, lover, musician and courtier, all with an equal nonchalance, permeates this play. Valentine and Proteus are sent to the Emperor's court principally to acquire this veneer. Indeed, the very story of the play, in common with several of Shakespeare's earlier pieces, is drawn from one of those Italian novelle which were shipped over to England, as an eminent Oxford academic once put it, 'by the boatload'. The scenes between Valentine and Silvia, and Valentine, Silvia and Proteus, in Act II can barely be performed at all without the realisation that, according to the courtly code, a verbal duel of wits between competing lovers was an important way of demonstrating devotion and winning the lady's favour.

But quite apart from the instances of *folie d'Italie* so clear in the play, there are several other crucial references to contemporary cultural fashions which recur in the text. The most obvious of these is the continuing reference to Marlowe's poem, *Hero and Leander*, which would have been circulating in manuscript for about a year at the time usually assigned for the writing of this play. There are several overt references to the myth, the first as early as the play's twenty-second line, seemingly announcing quite plainly that this play is going to be at least partly concerned with current questions concerning poets and poetry. *Hero and Leander*, with its openly homosexual second book and the luscious brilliance of its writing, had clearly swept the literary town, and in addition to the overt references – and the fact that the name 'Proteus' is almost certainly suggested by the description of the Temple of Venus in the poem where the shape-shifting God is mentioned by name – there are many other verbal echoes and cross-references to Marlowe's poem in Shakespeare's text. All through the play, jokes about writing poetry abound: Valentine's execrable sonnet to Silvia, a quatrain short, banal in thought and leaden-footed in execution – and, interestingly, loaded with Italianate feminine rhymes – is too long to be serving a merely dramatic purpose. The dramatic point could have been conveyed in two or three lines: but Shakespeare writes a full-length, or at least amputated, bad poem, as a joke, which he clearly expects his audience to share. Similarly, when Proteus instructs Thurio in the art of writing love poetry, he lists, surely tongue in cheek, all the most thunderous clichés of Elizabethan amorous verse; and Speed goes into plodding hexameters at one point, announcing, 'All this I speak in print, for in print I found it,' obviously making some contemporary reference now hopelessly lost to us. Finally, as if to summarise this continuing interest in poetry in the play, in Act IV Shakespeare gives Proteus one of the most perfectly-formed love lyrics in the language, 'Who is Silvia?'.

For the first two Acts of the play these fashionable themes are dominant. Then it seems almost as if Shakespeare is seized by the excitement of his theme of love and friendship and betrayal, so that the action, and its moral and ethical implications, and potential tragic outcome, become central, and the fashionable elements retreat into the background.

There is no way a director can convey to an audience literary and historical information which it does not possess. The best he or she can do is to attempt to suggest it, by the creation of a specific atmosphere. I decided to do this by trying to create in the design and staging of the play that dream world of the Italian Renaissance that is the essence of the mania for everything Italian in Elizabethan England, and to emphasise the artificiality of the early love scenes rather than trying to make them 'real' – which they could hardly ever be, and were surely never intended to be. The serious moral purpose even of so light a play is to show us how easily the frivolities of the game of love can turn sour and poison the players, resulting in tragedy or, at least, the possibilty of tragedy: in Act V we are within a few lines of a tragic outcome.

The dramatic and tragic elements of the play are easy for us to comprehend. It seemed to me that if I could get the first two Acts right, by the creation of an atmosphere of light-hearted games in a courtly landscape, the play's moral progress would reveal itself naturally, without the need either for heavy-handed underlining or ruthless cutting of the text.

No one knows how or when *Two Gentlemen* was written or in what circumstances it was performed. My own guess is that it was not intended for the public theatre, but like *Love's Labour's Lost* was written to entertain an audience of intelligent and educated young men, dramatising the issues of most moment to them, and the cultural fashions that were likely to constitute a good part of their conversation. Perhaps the play was written for the young men of the Inns of Court, or to delight and instruct the scions of some noble family. There is no evidence either way, and not likely to be. We have simply the text, to bring to life the best way we see fit.

It was my intention to perform the whole play, uncut. In the case of four or five famous cruces, I emended the text in order to make it comprehensible; and having cast a brown-eyed actress to play Julia, I cut the line in Act IV which states that her eyes are grey as glass. We did, experimentally, try coloured contact lenses in an effort to preserve Shakespeare's rhythm in a crucial speech: but that only made her look like a Martian, so we thought that in this case Shakespeare was best served by removing the whole line. As always, in the heat of performance, the actors made a few spontaneous emendations and transpositions of their own: otherwise, we played exactly what has come down to us from the Folio. After all, that is likely to have been put together from post-production copies of Shakespeare's originals, supervised by his fellow actors: and if you make the assumption that they are tried and oft-performed texts, created by a poet and company who knew from long experience what works and what doesn't, you are not likely to go very far wrong.

The production was not designed with any concern for naturalism. The set was open, covering the whole studio, and consisted of arches and columns, towers and balustrades, all mounted on floors painted to suggest ornamental marble, and backed by a permanent Tuscan blue sky. The area representing Verona was something between a courtyard and a garden, and Milan was suggested by a series of ornamental columns upon an octagonal dais, an archway, a fountain, a tower and colonnade, and the Garden of Love. There were no walls, except those supporting the towers. Proteus' study and Julia's room were suggested by arrangements of open arches, high upon rostra, with the rest of the set visible through and beyond them. It was therefore rare for a scene to be set in a clearly specified place.

*Tyler Butterworth as Proteus and (behind) John Hudson as Valentine*

# THE TWO GENTLEMEN OF VERONA

## DRAMATIS PERSONÆ

DUKE OF MILAN, *father to Silvia.*
VALENTINE, } *the two gentlemen.*
PROTEUS, }
ANTONIO, *father to Proteus.*
THURIO, *a foolish rival to Valentine.*
EGLAMOUR, *agent for Silvia in her escape.*
SPEED, *a clownish servant to Valentine.*
LAUNCE, *the like to Proteus.*
PANTHINO, *servant to Antonio.*

HOST, *where Julia lodges in Milan*
OUTLAWS, *with Valentine.*
JULIA, *a lady of Verona, beloved of Proteus.*
SILVIA, *the Duke's daughter, beloved of Valentine.*
LUCETTA, *waiting-woman to Julia.*
SERVANTS.
MUSICIANS.

THE SCENE : *Verona ; Milan ; the frontiers of Mantua.*

## ACT ONE.

SCENE I. *Verona. An open place.*

*Enter* VALENTINE *and* PROTEUS.

VAL. Cease to persuade, my loving Proteus :
Home-keeping youth have ever homely wits.
Were't not affection chains thy tender days
To the sweet glances of thy honour'd love,
I rather would entreat thy company                    5
To see the wonders of the world abroad,
Than, living dully sluggardiz'd at home,
Wear out thy youth with shapeless idleness.
But since thou lov'st, love still, and thrive therein,
Even as I would, when I to love begin.                 10
PRO. Wilt thou be gone ?  Sweet Valentine, adieu !
Think on thy Proteus, when thou haply seest
Some rare noteworthy object in thy travel.
Wish me partaker in thy happiness
When thou dost meet good hap ; and in thy danger,      15
If ever danger do environ thee,
Commend thy grievance to my holy prayers,
For I will be thy beadsman, Valentine.
VAL. And on a love-book pray for my success ?
PRO. Upon some book I love I'll pray for thee.         20
VAL. That's on some shallow story of deep love :
How young Leander cross'd the Hellespont.
PRO. That's a deep story of a deeper love ;
For he was more than over shoes in love.               25
VAL. 'Tis true ; for you are over boots in love,
And yet you never swum the Hellespont.

SCENE I
*Exterior. Verona.
Day.*
See note 1 (page 85).

SCENE 2
*Interior/Exterior.
Proteus' Study. Day*
See note 2 (page 85).

PRO. Over the boots ! Nay, give me not the boots.
VAL. No, I will not, for it boots thee not.
PRO. What ?
VAL. To be in love—where scorn is bought with groans,
    Coy looks with heart-sore sighs, one fading moment's mirth   30
    With twenty watchful, weary, tedious nights ;
    If haply won, perhaps a hapless gain ;
    If lost, why then a grievous labour won ;
    However, but a folly bought with wit,
    Or else a wit by folly vanquished.                   35
PRO. So, by your circumstance, you call me fool.
VAL. So, by your circumstance, I fear you'll prove.
PRO. 'Tis love you cavil at ; I am not Love.
VAL. Love is your master, for he masters you ,
    And he that is so yoked by a fool,               40
    Methinks, should not be chronicled for wise.
PRO. Yet writers say, as in the sweetest bud
    The eating canker dwells, so eating love
    Inhabits in the finest wits of all.
VAL. And writers say, as the most forward bud     45
    Is eaten by the canker ere it blow,
    Even so by love the young and tender wit
    Is turn'd to folly, blasting in the bud,
    Losing his verdure even in the prime,
    And all the fair effects of future hopes.     50
    But wherefore waste I time to counsel thee
    That art a votary to fond desire ?
    Once more adieu. My father at the road
    Expects my coming, there to see me shipp'd.
PRO. And thither will I bring thee, Valentine.     55
VAL. Sweet Proteus, no ; now let us take our leave.
    To Milan let me hear from thee by letters
    Of thy success in love, and what news else
    Betideth here in absence of thy friend ;
    And I likewise will visit thee with mine.     60
PRO. All happiness bechance to thee in Milan !
VAL. As much to you at home ; and so farewell !   [exit VALENTINE
PRO He after honour hunts, I after love ;
    He leaves his friends to dignify them more :
    I leave myself, my friends, and all for love.     65
    Thou, Julia, thou hast metamorphis'd me,
    Made me neglect my studies, lose my time,
    War with good counsel, set the world at nought :
    Made wit with musing weak, heart sick with thought.

*Enter* SPEED.

SPEED. Sir Proteus, save you ! Saw you my master ?     70
PRO. But now he parted hence to embark for Milan.
SPEED. Twenty to one then he is shipp'd already,
    And I have play'd the sheep in losing him.
PRO. Indeed a sheep doth very often stray,
    An if the shepherd be awhile away.     75
SPEED. You conclude that my master is a shepherd then, and I a sheep?
PRO. I do.

SPEED. Why then, my horns are his horns, whether I wake or sleep.
PRO. A silly answer, and fitting well a sheep.
SPEED. This proves me still a sheep.                                    80
PRO. True ; and thy master a shepherd.
SPEED. Nay, that I can deny by a circumstance.
PRO. It shall go hard but I'll prove it by another.
SPEED. The shepherd seeks the sheep, and not the sheep the shepherd ;
    but I seek my master, and my master seeks not me ; therefore,
    I am no sheep.                                                      86
PRO. The sheep for fodder follow the shepherd ; the shepherd for
    food follows not the sheep : thou for wages followest thy master ;
    thy master for wages follows not thee.   Therefore, thou art a
    sheep.                                                             90
SPEED. Such another proof will make me cry ' baa '.
PRO. But dost thou hear ?   Gav'st thou my letter to Julia ?
SPEED. Ay, sir ; I, a lost mutton, gave your letter to her, a lac'd
    mutton ; and she, a lac'd mutton, gave me, a lost mutton, nothing
    for my labour.                                                     96
PRO. Here's too small a pasture for such store of muttons.
SPEED. If the ground be overcharg'd, you were best stick her.
PRO. Nay, in that you are astray : 'twere best pound you.              100
SPEED. Nay, sir, less than a pound shall serve me for carrying your
    letter.
PRO. You mistake ; I mean the pound—a pinfold.
SPEED. From a pound to a pin ?   Fold it over and over,
    'Tis threefold too little for carrying a letter to your lover.     105
PRO. But what said she ?                                               See below* and
SPEED. [nodding.] Ay.                                                  note 3 (page 85).
PRO. Nod-ay.   Why, that's ' noddy '.
SPEED. You mistook, sir ; I say she did nod ; and you ask me if she
    did nod ; and I say ' Ay '.                                        110
PRO. And that set together is ' noddy '.
SPEED. Now you have taken the pains to set it together, take it for
    your pains.
PRO. No, no ; you shall have it for bearing the letter.
SPEED. Well, I perceive I must be fain to bear with you.               115
PRO. Why, sir, how do you bear with me ?
SPEED. Marry, sir, the letter, very orderly ; having nothing but the
    word ' noddy ' for my pains.
PRO. Beshrew me, but you have a quick wit.
SPEED. And yet it cannot overtake your slow purse.                     120
PRO. Come, come, open the matter ; in brief, what said she ?
SPEED. Open your purse, that the money and the matter may be both
    at once delivered.
PRO. Well, sir, here is for your pains.   What said she ?              125
SPEED. Truly, sir, I think you'll hardly win her.
PRO. Why, couldst thou perceive so much from her ?
SPEED. Sir, I could perceive nothing at all from her ; no, not so much
    as a ducat for delivering your letter ; and being so hard to me
    that brought your mind, I fear she'll prove as hard to you in
    telling your mind.   Give her no token but stones, for she's as
    hard as steel.                                                     132
PRO. What said she ?   Nothing ?
SPEED. No, not so much as ' Take this for thy pains '.   To testify

---

*Lines 106–108 spoken as follows:*
PRO. But what said she?
SPEED. Mmm. [nodding]
PRO. Mmm? [nodding]
SPEED. Ay.
PRO. Mmm, ay? Why, that's 'noddy'.

your bounty, I thank you, you have testern'd me ; in requital
whereof, henceforth carry your letters yourself ; and so, sir, I'll
commend you to my master.
PRO. Go, go, be gone, to save your ship from wreck,
Which cannot perish, having thee aboard,
Being destin'd to a drier death on shore.                    [*exit* SPEED.
I must go send some better messenger.                    141
I fear my Julia would not deign my lines,
Receiving them from such a worthless post.                    [*exit.*

SCENE II.    *Verona.    The garden of* JULIA'S *house.*

*Enter* JULIA *and* LUCETTA.

JUL.  But say, Lucetta, now we are alone,
Wouldst thou then counsel me to fall in love ?
LUC.  Ay, madam ; so you stumble not unheedfully.
JUL.  Of all the fair resort of gentlemen
That every day with parle encounter me,                    5
In thy opinion which is worthiest love ?
LUC.  Please you, repeat their names ; I'll show my mind
According to my shallow simple skill.
JUL.  What think'st thou of the fair Sir Eglamour ?
LUC.  As of a knight well-spoken, neat, and fine ;                    10
But, were I you, he never should be mine.
JUL.  What think'st thou of the rich Mercatio ?
LUC.  Well of his wealth ; but of himself, so so.
JUL.  What think'st thou of the gentle Proteus ?
LUC.  Lord, Lord ! to see what folly reigns in us !                    15
JUL.  How now ! what means this passion at his name ?
LUC.  Pardon, dear madam ; 'tis a passing shame
That I, unworthy body as I am,
Should censure thus on lovely gentlemen.
JUL.  Why not on Proteus, as of all the rest ?                    20
LUC.  Then thus : of many good I think him best.
JUL.  Your reason ?
LUC.  I have no other but a woman's reason :
I think him so, because I think him so.
JUL.  And wouldst thou have me cast my love on him ?                    25
LUC.  Ay, if you thought your love not cast away.
JUL.  Why, he, of all the rest, hath never mov'd me.
LUC.  Yet he, of all the rest, I think, best loves ye.
JUL.  His little speaking shows his love but small.
LUC.  Fire that's closest kept burns most of all.                    30
JUL.  They do not love that do not show their love.
LUC.  O, they love least that let men know their love.
JUL.  I would I knew his mind.
LUC.  Peruse this paper, madam.
JUL.  ' To Julia '—Say, from whom ?                    35
LUC.  That the contents will show.
JUL.  Say, say, who gave it thee ?
LUC.  Sir Valentine's page ; and sent, I think, from Proteus.
He would have given it you ; but I, being in the way,
Did in your name receive it ; pardon the fault, I pray                    40

SCENE 3
*Exterior. Verona.*
*Day.*
See note 4 (page 85).

SCENE 4
*Interior/Exterior.*
*Verona. Julia's Tower*
*Room. Day*

JUL. Now, by my modesty, a goodly broker!
  Dare you presume to harbour wanton lines?
  To whisper and conspire against my youth?
  Now, trust me, 'tis an office of great worth,
  And you an officer fit for the place.                                45
  There, take the paper; see it be return'd;
  Or else return no more into my sight.
LUC. To plead for love deserves more fee than hate.
JUL. Will ye be gone?
LUC.                          That you may ruminate.              [exit.
JUL. And yet, I would I had o'erlook'd the letter.                  50
  It were a shame to call her back again,
  And pray her to a fault for which I chid her.
  What fool is she, that knows I am a maid
  And would not force the letter to my view!
  Since maids, in modesty, say 'No' to that                         55
  Which they would have the profferer construe 'Ay'.
  Fie, fie, how wayward is this foolish love,
  That like a testy babe will scratch the nurse,
  And presently, all humbled, kiss the rod!
  How churlishly I chid Lucetta hence,                              60
  When willingly I would have had her here!
  How angerly I taught my brow to frown,
  When inward joy enforc'd my heart to smile
  My penance is to call Lucetta back
  And ask remission for my folly past.                              65
  What ho! Lucetta!

*Re-enter* LUCETTA.

LUC.                    What would your ladyship?
JUL. Is't near dinner time?
LUC.                    I would it were,
  That you might kill your stomach on your meat
  And not upon your maid.
JUL. What is't that you took up so gingerly?                        70
LUC. Nothing.
JUL. Why didst thou stoop then?
LUC. To take a paper up that I let fall.
JUL. And is that paper nothing?
LUC. Nothing concerning me.                                        75
JUL. Then let it lie for those that it concerns.
LUC. Madam, it will not lie where it concerns,
  Unless it have a false interpreter.
JUL. Some love of yours hath writ to you in rhyme,
LUC. That I might sing it, madam, to a tune.                        80
  Give me a note; your ladyship can set.
JUL. As little by such toys as may be possible.
  Best sing it to the tune of 'Light o' Love'.
LUC. It is too heavy for so light a tune.
JUL. Heavy! belike it hath some burden then.                       85
LUC. Ay; and melodious were it, would you sing it.
JUL. And why not you?
LUC.                    I cannot reach so high.

*Tessa Peake-Jones as Julia*

JUL. Let's see your song. [LUCETTA *withholds the letter.*] How now,
minion !
LUC. Keep tune there still, so you will sing it out.
And yet methinks I do not like this tune.                        90
JUL. You do not !
LUC.                        No, madam ; 'tis too sharp.
JUL. You, minion, are too saucy.
LUC. Nay, now you are too flat
And mar the concord with too harsh a descant ;
There wanteth but a mean to fill your song.                      95
JUL. The mean is drown'd with your unruly bass.
LUC. Indeed, I bid the base for Proteus.
JUL. This babble shall not henceforth trouble me.
Here is a coil with protestation !          [*tears the letter.*
Go, get you gone ; and let the papers lie.                      100
You would be fing'ring them, to anger me.
LUC. She makes it strange ; but she would be best pleas'd
To be so ang'red with another letter.              [*exit.*
JUL. Nay, would I were so ang'red with the same !
O hateful hands, to tear such loving words !                    105
Injurious wasps, to feed on such sweet honey
And kill the bees that yield it with your stings !
I'll kiss each several paper for amends.
Look, here is writ ' kind Julia '. Unkind Julia,
As in revenge of thy ingratitude,                               110
I throw thy name against the bruising stones,
Trampling contemptuously on thy disdain.
And here is writ ' love-wounded Proteus '.
Poor wounded name ! my bosom, as a bed,
Shall lodge thee till thy wound be throughly heal'd             115
And thus I search it with a sovereign kiss.
But twice or thrice was ' Proteus ' written down.
Be calm, good wind, blow not a word away
Till I have found each letter in the letter—
Except mine own name ; that some whirlwind bear                 120
Unto a ragged, fearful, hanging rock,
And throw it thence into the raging sea.
Lo, here in one line is his name twice writ :
' Poor forlorn Proteus, passionate Proteus,
To the sweet Julia '. That I'll tear away ;                     125
And yet I will not, sith so prettily
He couples it to his complaining names.
Thus will I fold them one upon another ;
Now kiss, embrace, contend, do what you will.

*Re-enter* LUCETTA.

LUC. Madam,                                                      130
Dinner is ready, and your father stays.
JUL. Well, let us go.
LUC. What, shall these papers lie like tell-tales here ?
JUL. If you respect them, best to take them up.
LUC. Nay, I was taken up for laying them down ;                 135
Yet here they shall not lie for catching cold.
JUL. I see you have a month's mind to them.

LUC. Ay, madam, you may say what sights you see
  I see things too, although you judge I wink.          139
JUL. Come, come ; will't please you go ?          [*exeunt.*

SCENE III. *Verona.* ANTONIO'S *house.*

*Enter* ANTONIO *and* PANTHINO.

SCENE 5
*Interior/Exterior.*
*Verona. Evening.*
See note 5 (page 85).

ANT. Tell me, Panthino, what sad talk was that
  Wherewith my brother held you in the cloister ?
PAN. 'Twas of his nephew Proteus, your son.
ANT. Why, what of him ?
PAN.          He wond'red that your lordship
  Would suffer him to spend his youth at home,          5
  While other men, of slender reputation,
  Put forth their sons to seek preferment out :
  Some to the wars, to try their fortune there ;
  Some to discover islands far away ;
  Some to the studious universities.          10
  For any, or for all these exercises,
  He said that Proteus, your son, was meet ;
  And did request me to importune you
  To let him spend his time no more at home,
  Which would be great impeachment to his age,          15
  In having known no travel in his youth.
ANT. Nor need'st thou much importune me to that
  Whereon this month I have been hammering.
  I have consider'd well his loss of time,
  And how he cannot be a perfect man,          20
  Not being tried and tutor'd in the world :
  Experience is by industry achiev'd,
  And perfected by the swift course of time.
  Then tell me whither were I best to send him.
PAN. I think your lordship is not ignorant          25
  How his companion, youthful Valentine,
  Attends the Emperor in his royal court.
ANT. I know it well.
PAN. 'Twere good, I think, your lordship sent him thither :
  There shall he practise tilts and tournaments,          30
  Hear sweet discourse, converse with noblemen,
  And be in eye of every exercise
  Worthy his youth and nobleness of birth.
ANT. I like thy counsel ; well hast thou advis'd ;
  And that thou mayst perceive how well I like it,          35
  The execution of it shall make known :
  Even with the speediest expedition
  I will dispatch him to the Emperor's court.
PAN. To-morrow, may it please you, Don Alphonso
  With other gentlemen of good esteem          40
  Are journeying to salute the Emperor,
  And to commend their service to his will.
ANT. Good company ; with them shall Proteus go.

*Enter* PROTEUS.

44

And—in good time !—now will we break with him.
PRO. Sweet love ! sweet lines ! sweet life !                                45
Here is her hand, the agent of her heart ;
Here is her oath for love, her honour's pawn.
O that our fathers would applaud our loves,
To seal our happiness with their consents !
O heavenly Julia !                                                          50
ANT. How now ! What letter are you reading there ?
PRO. May't please your lordship, 'tis a word or two
Of commendations sent from Valentine,
Deliver'd by a friend that came from him.
ANT. Lend me the letter ; let me see what news.                             55
PRO. There is no news, my lord ; but that he writes
How happily he lives, how well-belov'd
And daily graced by the Emperor ;
Wishing me with him, partner of his fortune.
ANT. And how stand you affected to his wish ?                               60
PRO. As one relying on your lordship's will,
And not depending on his friendly wish.
ANT. My will is something sorted with his wish.
Muse not that I thus suddenly proceed ;
For what I will, I will, and there an end.                                  65
I am resolv'd that thou shalt spend some time
With Valentinus in the Emperor's court ;
What maintenance he from his friends receives,
Like exhibition thou shalt have from me.
To-morrow be in readiness to go—                                           70
Excuse it not, for I am peremptory.
PRO. My lord, I cannot be so soon provided ;
Please you, deliberate a day or two.
ANT. Look what thou want'st shall be sent after thee.
No more of stay ; to-morrow thou must go.                                   75
Come on, Panthino ; you shall be employ'd
To hasten on his expedition.
                              [*exeunt* ANTONIO *and* PANTHINO.
PRO. Thus have I shunn'd the fire for fear of burning,
And drench'd me in the sea, where I am drown'd.
I fear'd to show my father Julia's letter,                                  80
Lest he should take exceptions to my love ;
And with the vantage of mine own excuse
Hath he excepted most against my love.
O, how this spring of love resembleth
The uncertain glory of an April day,                                        85
Which now shows all the beauty of the sun,
And by and by a cloud takes all away !

                    *Re-enter* PANTHINO.

PAN. Sir Proteus, your father calls for you ;
He is in haste ; therefore, I pray you, go.
PRO. Why, this it is : my heart accords thereto ;                           90
And yet a thousand times it answers ' No '.                 [*exeunt.*

SCENE 6
*Interior/Exterior.*
*Verona. Evening.*
PROTEUS in his study
alone. ANTONIO and
PANTHINO in the
courtyard below.
See note 6 (page 86).

The lutenist plays and
sings. See note 7
(page 86).

45

ACT TWO.

SCENE I.   *Milan.   The* DUKE'S *palace.*

*Enter* VALENTINE *and* SPEED.

SCENE 7
*Exterior. Milan. The
Garden of Love. Day.*
See note 8 (page 86).

SPEED. Sir, your glove.
VAL.                         Not mine : my gloves are on.
SPEED. Why, then, this may be yours ; for this is but one.
VAL. Ha ! let me see ; ay, give it me, it's mine ;
    Sweet ornament that decks a thing divine !
    Ah, Silvia ! Silvia !                                          5
SPEED. [*calling.*] Madam Silvia ! Madam Silvia !
VAL. How now, sirrah ?
SPEED. She is not within hearing, sir.
VAL. Why, sir, who bade you call her ?
SPEED. Your worship, sir ; or else I mistook.             10
VAL. Well, you'll still be too forward.
SPEED. And yet I was last chidden for being too slow.
VAL. Go to, sir ; tell me, do you know Madam Silvia ?
SPEED. She that your worship loves ?
VAL. Why, how know you that I am in love ?                15
SPEED. Marry, by these special marks : first, you have learn'd, like
    Sir Proteus, to wreath your arms like a malcontent ; to relish a
    love-song, like a robin redbreast ; to walk alone, like one that
    had the pestilence ; to sigh, like a school-boy that had lost his
    A B C ; to weep, like a young wench that had buried her
    grandam ; to fast, like one that takes diet ; to watch, like one that
    fears robbing ; to speak puling, like a beggar at Hallowmas.
    You were wont, when you laughed, to crow like a cock ; when you
    walk'd, to walk like one of the lions ; when you fasted, it was
    presently after dinner ; when you look'd sadly, it was for want of
    money.  And now you are metamorphis'd with a mistress, that,
    when I look on you, I can hardly think you my master.
VAL. Are all these things perceiv'd in me ?
SPEED. They are all perceiv'd without ye.                 30
VAL. Without me ? They cannot.
SPEED. Without you ! Nay, that's certain ; for, without you were so
    simple, none else would ; but you are so without these follies that
    these follies are within you, and shine through you like the water
    in an urinal, that not an eye that sees you but is a physician to
    comment on your malady.                                        36
VAL. But tell me, dost thou know my lady Silvia ?
SPEED. She that you gaze on so, as she sits at supper ?
VAL. Hast thou observ'd that ? Even she, I mean.
SPEED. Why, sir, I know her not.                          40
VAL. Dost thou know her by my gazing on her, and yet know'st her
    not ?
SPEED. Is she not hard-favour'd, sir ?
VAL. Not so fair, boy, as well-favour'd.
SPEED. Sir, I know that well enough.                       45
VAL. What dost thou know ?
SPEED. That she is not so fair as, of you, well favour'd.
VAL. I mean that her beauty is exquisite, but her favour infinite.

46

SPEED. That's because the one is painted, and the other out of all
    count.                                                                    51
VAL. How painted ? and how out of count ?
SPEED. Marry, sir, so painted, to make her fair, that no man counts of
    her beauty.
VAL. How esteem'st thou me ?   I account of her beauty.          55
SPEED. You never saw her since she was deform'd.
VAL. How long hath she been deform'd ?
SPEED. Ever since you lov'd her.
VAL. I have lov'd her ever since I saw her, and still I see her beautiful.
SPEED. If you love her, you cannot see her.                        61
VAL. Why ?
SPEED. Because Love is blind.   O that you had mine eyes ; or your
    own eyes had the lights they were wont to have when you chid at
    Sir Proteus for going ungarter'd !                             65
VAL. What should I see then ?
SPEED. Your own present folly and her passing deformity ;  for he,
    being in love, could not see to garter his hose ;  and you, being in
    love, cannot see to put on your hose.
VAL. Belike, boy, then you are in love ;  for last morning you could
    not see to wipe my shoes.                                      71
SPEED. True, sir ;  I was in love with my bed.   I thank you, you
    swing'd me for my love, which makes me the bolder to chide you
    for yours.
VAL. In conclusion, I stand affected to her.                       75
SPEED. I would you were set, so your affection would cease.
VAL. Last night she enjoin'd me to write some lines to one she loves.
SPEED. And have you ?                                              80
VAL. I have.
SPEED. Are they not lamely writ ?
VAL. No, boy, but as well as I can do them.

                        *Enter* SILVIA.

    Peace !  here she comes.
SPEED. [*aside*.]  O excellent motion !  O exceeding puppet !  Now
    will he interpret to her.                                      86
VAL. Madam and mistress, a thousand good morrows.
SPEED. [*aside*.]   O, give ye good ev'n !
    Here's a million of manners.
SIL. Sir Valentine and servant, to you two thousand.              90
SPEED. [*aside*.]  He should give her interest, and she gives it him.
VAL. As you enjoin'd me, I have writ your letter
    Unto the secret nameless friend of yours ;
    Which I was much unwilling to proceed in,                      95
    But for my duty to your ladyship.
SIL. I thank you, gentle servant.  'Tis very clerkly done.
VAL. Now trust me, madam, it came hardly off ;
    For, being ignorant to whom it goes,
    I writ at random, very doubtfully.                             100
SIL. Perchance you think too much of so much pains ?
VAL. No, madam ;  so it stead you, I will write,
    Please you command, a thousand times as much ;
    And yet—
SIL. A pretty period !  Well, I guess the sequel ;               105

To lute music, and
showered with rose
petals by the two
cupids.

And yet I will not name it—and yet I care not.
And yet take this again—and yet I thank you—
Meaning henceforth to trouble you no more.
SPEED. [*aside*.] And yet you will ; and yet another ' yet '.
VAL. What means your ladyship ? Do you not like it ? 110
SIL. Yes, yes ; the lines are very quaintly writ ;
But, since unwillingly, take them again.
Nay, take them. [*Gives back the letter.*
VAL. Madam, they are for you.
SIL. Ay, ay, you writ them, sir, at my request ; 115
But I will none of them ; they are for you :
I would have had them writ more movingly.
VAL. Please you, I'll write your ladyship another.
SIL. And when it's writ, for my sake read it over ;
And if it please you, so ; if not, why, so. 120
VAL. If it please me, madam, what then ?
SIL. Why, if it please you, take it for your labour.
And so good morrow, servant. [*exit* SILVIA.
SPEED. O jest unseen, inscrutable, invisible,
As a nose on a man's face, or a weathercock on a steeple ! 125
My master sues to her ; and she hath taught her suitor,
He being her pupil, to become her tutor.
O excellent device ! Was there ever heard a better,
That my master, being scribe, to himself should write the etter ?
VAL. How now, sir ! What are you reasoning with yourself ? 131
SPEED. Nay, I was rhyming : 'tis you that have the reason.
VAL. To do what ?
SPEED. To be a spokesman from Madam Silvia ? 135
VAL. To whom ?
SPEED. To yourself ; why, she woos you by a figure.
VAL. What figure ?
SPEED. By a letter, I should say.
VAL. Why, she hath not writ to me. 140
SPEED. What need she, when she hath made you write to yourself ?
Why, do you not perceive the jest ?
VAL. No, believe me.
SPEED. No believing you indeed, sir. But did you perceive her
earnest ? 145
VAL. She gave me none except an angry word.
SPEED. Why, she hath given you a letter.
VAL. That's the letter I writ to her friend.
SPEED. And that letter hath she deliver'd, and there an end. 150
VAL. I would it were no worse.
SPEED. I'll warrant you 'tis as well.
' For often have you writ to her ; and she, in modesty,
Or else for want of idle time, could not again reply ;
Or fearing else some messenger that might her mind discover,
Herself hath taught her love himself to write unto her lover.' 156
All this I speak in print, for in print I found it. Why muse you,
sir ? 'Tis dinner time.
VAL. I have din'd. 159
SPEED. Ay, but hearken, sir ; though the chameleon Love can feed
on the air, I am one that am nourish'd by my victuals, and would

fain have meat.   O, be not like your mistress !   Be moved, be
moved.                                                                                 [*exeunt.*

The two cupids wave
goodbye as SPEED and
VALENTINE leave the
Garden of Love.

SCENE II.   *Verona.*   JULIA'S *house.*

*Enter* PROTEUS *and* JULIA.

SCENE 8
*Interior/Exterior.*
*Verona. Proteus' Study.*
*Day.*
PROTEUS and JULIA are
saying goodbye.

PRO.  Have patience, gentle Julia.
JUL.  I must, where is no remedy.
PRO.  When possibly I can, I will return.
JUL.  If you turn not, you will return the sooner.
      Keep this remembrance for thy Julia's sake.        [*giving a ring.*
PRO.  Why, then, we'll make exchange.   Here, take you this.
JUL.  And seal the bargain with a holy kiss.
PRO.  Here is my hand for my true constancy ;
      And when that hour o'erslips me in the day
      Wherein I sigh not, Julia, for thy sake,                                10
      The next ensuing hour some foul mischance
      Torment me for my love's forgetfulness !
      My father stays my coming ; answer not ;
      The tide is now—nay, not thy tide of tears :
      That tide will stay me longer than I should.                           15
      Julia, farewell !                                              [*exit* JULIA.
                          What, gone without a word ?
      Ay, so true love should do : it cannot speak ;
      For truth hath better deeds than words to grace it.

*Enter* PANTHINO.

PAN.  Sir Proteus, you are stay'd for.
PRO.  Go ;  I come, I come.                                                   20
      Alas ! this parting strikes poor lovers dumb.             [*exeunt.*

PANTHINO enters in the
courtyard below and
calls up to them.

SCENE III.   *Verona.*   *A street.*

*Enter* LAUNCE, *leading a dog.*

As JULIA goes, LAUNCE
comes into the
courtyard below with
his dog and sits on the
steps.

LAUN.  Nay, 'twill be this hour ere I have done weeping ; all the kind
of the Launces have this very fault.   I have receiv'd my proportion, like the Prodigious Son, and am going with Sir Proteus
to the Imperial's court.   I think Crab my dog be the sourest-
natured dog that lives : my mother weeping, my father wailing,
my sister crying, our maid howling, our cat wringing her hands,
and all our house in a great perplexity ; yet did not this cruel-
hearted cur shed one tear.   He is a stone, a very pebble stone, and
has no more pity in him than a dog.   A Jew would have wept to
have seen our parting ; why, my grandam having no eyes, look
you, wept herself blind at my parting.   Nay, I'll show you the
manner of it.   This shoe is my father ; no, this left shoe is my
father ; no, no, this left shoe is my mother ; nay, that cannot be
so neither ; yes, it is so, it is so, it hath the worser sole.   This
shoe with the hole in it is my mother, and this my father.   A
vengeance on 't !   There 'tis.   Now, sir, this staff is my sister, for,
look you, she is as white as a lily and as small as a wand ; this hat
is Nan our maid ; I am the dog ; no, the dog is himself, and I am
the dog—O, the dog is me, and I am myself ; ay, so, so.   Now

| 'and all . . . perplexity'
omitted.

| 'and this my father'
omitted.

49

come I to my father : ' Father, your blessing '. Now should not
the shoe speak a word for weeping ; now should I kiss my father ;
well, he weeps on. Now come I to my mother. O that she could
speak now like a wood woman ! Well, I kiss her—why there 'tis ;
here's my mother's breath up and down. Now come I to my
sister ; mark the moan she makes. Now the dog all this while
sheds not a tear, nor speaks a word ; but see how I lay the dust
with my tears. 29

*See below\* and note 9
(page 86).*

*Enter* PANTHINO.

PAN. Launce, away, away aboard ! Thy master is shipp'd,
and thou art to post after with oars. What's the matter ? Why
weep'st thou, man ? Away, ass ! You'll lose the tide if you
tarry any longer.
LAUN. It is no matter if the tied were lost ; for it is the unkindest tied
that ever any man tied. 35
PAN. What's the unkindest tide ?
LAUN. Why, he that's tied here, Crab, my dog.
PAN. Tut, man, I mean thou'lt lose the flood, and, in losing the flood,
lose thy voyage, and, in losing thy voyage, lose thy master, and,
in losing thy master, lose thy service, and, in losing thy service—
Why dost thou stop my mouth ?
LAUN. For fear thou shouldst lose thy tongue. 42
PAN. Where should I lose my tongue ?
LAUN. In thy tale.
PAN. In thy tail ! 45
LAUN. Lose the tide, and the voyage, and the master, and the service,
and the tied ! Why, man, if the river were dry, I am able to fill it
with my tears ; if the wind were down, I could drive the boat with
my sighs.
PAN. Come, come away, man ; I was sent to call thee.
LAUN. Sir, call me what thou dar'st. 51
PAN. Wilt thou go ?
LAUN. Well, I will go. [*exeunt.*

SCENE IV. *Milan. The* DUKE'S *palace.*

*Enter* SILVIA, VALENTINE, THURIO, *and* SPEED.

SIL. Servant !
VAL. Mistress ?
SPEED. Master, Sir Thurio frowns on you.
VAL. Ay, boy, it's for love.
SPEED. Not of you. 5
VAL. Of my mistress, then.
SPEED. 'Twere good you knock'd him. [*exit.*
SIL. Servant, you are sad.
VAL. Indeed, madam, I seem so.
THU. Seem you that you are not ? 10
VAL. Haply I do.
THU. So do counterfeits.
VAL. So do you.
THU. What seem I that I am not ?
VAL. Wise. 15
THU. What instance of the contrary ?

*SCENE 9
Exterior. Milan. The
Garden of Love. Day.
See note 10 (page 86).*

SPEED *remains*

---

\*'weeping like a wild woman. Now shall I kiss my mother' spoken for 'like a
wood woman. Well, I kiss her'.

*Valentine (John Hudson) and Speed (Nicholas Kaby, extreme left) listen to the lutenists in the Garden of Love*

*Thurio (David Collings) and Valentine (John Hudson) sit with Silvia (Joanne Pearce) in the Garden of Love, watched by a golden Cupid*

VAL. Your folly.
THU. And how quote you my folly?
VAL. I quote it in your jerkin.
THU. My jerkin is a doublet.                                    20
VAL. Well, then, I'll double your folly.
THU. How?
SIL. What, angry, Sir Thurio! Do you change colour?
VAL. Give him leave, madam; he is a kind of chameleon.
THU. That hath more mind to feed on your blood than live in your air.
VAL. You have said, sir.                                        27
THU. Ay, sir, and done too, for this time.
VAL. I know it well, sir; you always end ere you begin.
SIL. A fine volley of words, gentlemen, and quickly shot off.   31
VAL. 'Tis indeed, madam; we thank the giver.
SIL. Who is that, servant?
VAL. Yourself, sweet lady; for you gave the fire. Sir Thurio
    borrows his wit from your ladyship's looks, and spends what he
    borrows kindly in your company.                            36
THU. Sir, if you spend word for word with me, I shall make your
    wit bankrupt.
VAL. I know it well, sir; you have an exchequer of words, and, I
    think, no other treasure to give your followers; for it appears by
    their bare liveries that they live by your bare words.      42

*Enter* DUKE

SIL. No more, gentlemen, no more. Here comes my father.
DUKE. Now, daughter Silvia, you are hard beset.                 45
    Sir Valentine, your father is in good health.
    What say you to a letter from your friends
    Of much good news?
VAL.                         My lord, I will be thankful
    To any happy messenger from thence.
DUKE. Know ye Don Antonio, your countryman?                     50
VAL. Ay, my good lord, I know the gentleman
    To be of worth and worthy estimation,
    And not without desert so well reputed.
DUKE. Hath he not a son?
VAL. Ay, my good lord; a son that well deserves                 55
    The honour and regard of such a father.
DUKE. You know him well?
VAL. I knew him as myself; for from our infancy
    We have convers'd and spent our hours together;
    And though myself have been an idle truant,                 60
    Omitting the sweet benefit of time
    To clothe mine age with angel-like perfection,
    Yet hath Sir Proteus, for that's his name,
    Made use and fair advantage of his days:
    His years but young, but his experience old;                65
    His head unmellowed, but his judgment ripe;
    And, in a word, for far behind his worth
    Comes all the praises that I now bestow,
    He is complete in feature and in mind,
    With all good grace to grace a gentleman.                   70
DUKE. Beshrew me, sir, but if he make this good,

*Hetta Charnley as Lucetta and Frank Barrie as Sir Eglamour*

*John Hudson as Valentine and Tyler Butterworth as Proteus*

*Hetta Charnley as Lucetta and Tessa Peake-Jones as Julia*

*Paul Daneman as the Duke of Milan*

*David Collings as Thurio*

*Nicholas Kaby as Speed and Tony Haygarth as Launce*

*Julia (Tessa Peake-Jones) disguised as a page*

*Joanne Pearce as Silvia*

*Silvia (Joanne Pearce) listens to Proteus singing 'Who is Silvia?'*

*Valentine (John Hudson) and Speed (Nicholas Kaby) are ambushed by the outlaws*

He is as worthy for an empress' love
As meet to be an emperor's counsellor.
Well, sir, this gentleman is come to me
With commendation from great potentates,                    75
And here he means to spend his time awhile.
I think 'tis no unwelcome news to you.
VAL. Should I have wish'd a thing, it had been he.
DUKE. Welcome him, then, according to his worth—
Silvia, I speak to you, and you, Sir Thurio;                80
For Valentine, I need not cite him to it.
I will send him hither to you presently.          [exit DUKE.     SPEED exits also.
VAL. This is the gentlemen I told your ladyship
Had come along with me but that his mistress
Did hold his eyes lock'd in her crystal looks.             85
SIL. Belike that now she hath enfranchis'd them
Upon some other pawn for fealty.
VAL. Nay, sure, I think she holds them prisoners still.
SIL. Nay, then, he should be blind; and, being blind,
How could he see his way to seek out you?                  90
VAL. Why, lady, Love hath twenty pair of eyes.
THU. They say that Love hath not an eye at all.
VAL. To see such lovers, Thurio, as yourself;
Upon a homely object Love can wink.          [exit THURIO.

*Enter* PROTEUS.

SIL. Have done, have done; here comes the gentleman.        95
VAL. Welcome, dear Proteus! Mistress, I beseech you
Confirm his welcome with some special favour.
SIL. His worth is warrant for his welcome hither.
If this be he you oft have wish'd to hear from.
VAL. Mistress, it is; sweet lady, entertain him           100
To be my fellow-servant to your ladyship.
SIL. Too low a mistress for so high a servant.
PRO. Not so, sweet lady; but too mean a servant
To have a look of such a worthy mistress.
VAL. Leave off discourse of disability;                   105
Sweet lady, entertain him for your servant.
PRO. My duty will I boast of, nothing else.
SIL. And duty never yet did want his meed.
Servant, you are welcome to a worthless mistress.
PRO. I'll die on him that says so but yourself.           110
SIL. That you are welcome?
PRO.                    That you are worthless.

*Re-enter* THURIO.

THU. Madam, my lord your father would speak with you.
SIL. I wait upon his pleasure. Come, Sir Thurio,
Go with me. Once more, new servant, welcome.
I'll leave you to confer of home affairs;                 115
When you have done we look to hear from you.
PRO. We'll both attend upon your ladyship.
                              [*exeunt* SILVIA *and* THURIO.
VAL. Now, tell me, how do all from whence you came?
PRO. Your friends are well, and have them much commended.

VAL. And how do yours?
PRO.                          I left them all in health.           120
VAL. How does your lady, and how thrives your love?
PRO. My tales of love were wont to weary you;
   I know you joy not in a love-discourse.
VAL. Ay, Proteus, but that life is alter'd now;
   I have done penance for contemning Love,              125
   Whose high imperious thoughts have punish'd me
   With bitter fasts, with penitential groans,
   With nightly tears, and daily heart-sore sighs;
   For, in revenge of my contempt of love,
   Love hath chas'd sleep from my enthralled eyes        130
   And made them watchers of mine own heart's sorrow.
   O gentle Proteus, Love's a mighty lord,
   And hath so humbled me as I confess
   There is no woe to his correction,
   Nor to his service no such joy on earth.              135
   Now no discourse, except it be of love;
   Now can I break my fast, dine, sup, and sleep,
   Upon the very naked name of love.
PRO. Enough; I read your fortune in your eye.
   Was this the idol that you worship so?                140
VAL. Even she; and is she not a heavenly saint?
PRO. No; but she is an earthly paragon.
VAL. Call her divine.
PRO.                          I will not flatter her.
VAL. O, flatter me; for love delights in praises!
PRO. When I was sick you gave me bitter pills,           145
   And I must minister the like to you.
VAL. Then speak the truth by her; if not divine,
   Yet let her be a principality,
   Sovereign to all the creatures on the earth.
PRO. Except my mistress.
VAL.                          Sweet, except not any;       150
   Except thou wilt except against my love.
PRO. Have I not reason to prefer mine own?
VAL. And I will help thee to prefer her too:
   She shall be dignified with this high honour—
   To bear my lady's train, lest the base earth          155
   Should from her vesture chance to steal a kiss
   And, of so great a favour growing proud,
   Disdain to root the summer-swelling flow'r
   And make rough winter everlastingly.
PRO. Why, Valentine, what braggardism is this?           160
VAL. Pardon me, Proteus; all I can is nothing
   To her, whose worth makes other worthies nothing;
   She is alone.
PRO.                          Then let her alone.
VAL. Not for the world! Why, man, she is mine own;
   And I as rich in having such a jewel                  165
   As twenty seas, if all their sand were pearl,
   The water nectar, and the rocks pure gold.
   Forgive me that I do not dream on thee,
   Because thou seest me dote upon my love.

My foolish rival, that her father likes                    170
Only for his possessions are so huge,
Is gone with her along ; and I must after,
For love, thou know'st, is full of jealousy.
PRO. But she loves you ?
VAL. Ay, and we are betroth'd ; nay more, our marriage-hour,   175
With all the cunning manner of our flight,
Determin'd of—how I must climb her window,
The ladder made of cords, and all the means
Plotted and 'greed on for my happiness.
Good Proteus, go with me to my chamber,                    180
In these affairs to aid me with thy counsel.
PRO. Go on before ; I shall enquire you forth ;
I must unto the road to disembark
Some necessaries that I needs must use ;
And then I'll presently attend you.                        185
VAL. Will you make haste ?
PRO. I will.                          [exit VALENTINE    See note 11 (page 87).
Even as one heat another heat expels
Or as one nail by strength drives out another,
So the remembrance of my former love                       190
Is by a newer object quite forgotten.
Is it my mind, or Valentinus' praise,
Her true perfection, or my false transgression,
That makes me reasonless to reason thus ?
She is fair ; and so is Julia that I love—                 195
That I did love, for now my love is thaw'd ;
Which like a waxen image 'gainst a fire
Bears no  impression of the thing it was.
Methinks my zeal to Valentine is cold,
And that I love him not as I was wont.                      200
O ! but I love his lady too too much,
And that's the reason I love him so little.
How shall I dote on her with more advice
That thus without advice begin to love her!
'Tis but her picture I have yet beheld,                     205
And that hath dazzled my reason's light ;
But when I look on her perfections,
There is no reason but I shall be blind.
If I can check my erring love, I will ;                     209
If not, to compass her I'll use my skill.                  [exit.

SCENE V. *Milan.  A street.*

*Enter* SPEED *and* LAUNCE *severally.*

SCENE 10
Exterior. Milan. Day.
'the court' for 'Padua'.
See note 12 (page 87).

SPEED. Launce ! by mine honesty, welcome to Padua.
LAUN. Forswear not thyself, sweet youth, for I am not welcome. I
reckon this always, that a man is never undone till he be hang'd,
nor never welcome to a place till some certain shot be paid, and
the hostess say ' Welcome ! '                              5
SPEED. Come on, you madcap ; I'll to the alehouse with you presently;
where, for one shot of five pence, thou shalt have five thousand
welcomes. But, sirrah, how did thy master part with Madam
Julia ?                                                    9

*Valentine (John Hudson) watches the meeting of Proteus (Tyler Butterworth) and Silvia (Joanne Pearce)*

*Nicholas Kaby as Speed and Tony Haygarth as Launce*

LAUN. Marry, after they clos'd in earnest, they parted very fairly
   in jest.
SPEED. But shall she marry him?
LAUN. No.
SPEED. How then?  Shall he marry her?
LAUN. No. neither.                                               15
SPEED. What, are they broken?
LAUN. No. they are both as whole as a fish.
SPEED  Why then, how stands the matter with them?
LAUN. Marry, thus :  when it stands well with him, it stands well
   with her.                                                    20
SPEED. What an ass art thou!  I understand thee not.
LAUN. What a block art thou that thou canst not!  My staff under-
   stands me.                                                   26
SPEED. What thou say'st?
LAUN. Ay, and what I do too :  look thee, I'll but lean, and my staff
   understands me.
SPEED. It stands under thee, indeed.
LAUN. Why, stand-under and under-stand is all one.
SPEED. But tell me true, will't be a match?
LAUN. Ask my dog.  If he say ay, it will ; if he say no, it will ; if he
   shake his tail and say nothing, it will.
SPEED. The conclusion is, then, that it will.                   32
LAUN. Thou shalt never get such a secret from me but by a parable.
SPEED. 'Tis well that I get it so.  But, Launce, how say'st thou that
   my master is become a notable lover?
LAUN. I never knew him otherwise.
SPEED. Than how?
LAUN. A notable lubber, as thou reportest him to be.
SPEED. Why, thou whoreson ass, thou mistak'st me.               40
LAUN. Why, fool, I meant not thee, I meant thy master.
SPEED. I tell thee my master is become a hot lover.
LAUN. Why, I tell thee I care not though he burn himself in love.
   If thou wilt, go with me to the alehouse ; if not, thou art an
   Hebrew, a Jew, and not worth the name of a Christian.        46
SPEED. Why?
LAUN. Because thou hast not so much charity in thee as to go to the
   ale with a Christian.  Wilt thou go?
SPEED. At thy service                                     [exeunt.

SCENE VI.   *Milan.   The* DUKE'S *palace.*

*Enter* PROTEUS.

PRO. To leave my Julia, shall I be forsworn ;
   To love fair Silvia, shall I be forsworn ;
   To wrong my friend, I shall be much forsworn ;
   And ev'n that pow'r which gave me first my oath
   Provokes me to this threefold perjury :                       5
   Love bade me swear, and Love bids me forswear.
   O sweet-suggesting Love, if thou hast sinn'd,
   Teach me, thy tempted subject, to excuse it!
   At first I did adore a twinkling star,
   But now I worship a celestial sun.                           10
   Unheedful vows may heedfully be broken ;

SCENE II
*Exterior. Milan. The
Garden of Love. Day*

57

And he wants wit that wants resolved will
To learn his wit t' exchange the bad for better.
Fie, fie, unreverent tongue, to call her bad
Whose sovereignty so oft thou hast preferr'd                15
With twenty thousand soul-confirming oaths!
I cannot leave to love, and yet I do;
But there I leave to love where I should love.
Julia I lose, and Valentine I lose;
If I keep them, I needs must lose myself;                   20
If I lose them, thus find I by their loss:
For Valentine, myself; for Julia, Silvia.
I to myself am dearer than a friend;
For love is still most precious in itself;
And Silvia—witness heaven, that made her fair!—             25
Shows Julia but a swarthy Ethiope.
I will forget that Julia is alive,
Rememb'ring that my love to her is dead;
And Valentine I'll hold an enemy,
Aiming at Silvia as a sweeter friend.                       30
I cannot now prove constant to myself
Without some treachery us'd to Valentine.
This night he meaneth with a corded ladder
To climb celestial Silvia's chamber window,
Myself in counsel, his competitor.                          35
Now presently I'll give her father notice
Of their disguising and pretended flight,
Who, all enrag'd, will banish Valentine,
For Thurio, he intends, shall wed his daughter;
But, Valentine being gone, I'll quickly cross               40
By some sly trick blunt Thurio's dull proceeding.
Love, lend me wings to make my purpose swift,
As thou hast lent me wit to plot this drift.            [exit.

SCENE VII. *Verona.* JULIA'S *house.*

*Enter* JULIA *and* LUCETTA.

JUL. Counsel, Lucetta; gentle girl, assist me;
And, ev'n in kind love, I do conjure thee,
Who art the table wherein all my thoughts
Are visibly character'd and engrav'd,
To lesson me and tell me some good mean                      5
How, with my honour, I may undertake
A journey to my loving Proteus.
LUC. Alas, the way is wearisome and long!
JUL. A true-devoted pilgrim is not weary
To measure kingdoms with his feeble steps;                  10
Much less shall she that hath Love's wings to fly,
And when the flight is made to one so dear,
Of such divine perfection, as Sir Proteus.
LUC. Better forbear till Proteus make return.
JUL. O, know'st thou not his looks are my soul's food?      15
Pity the dearth that I have pined in
By longing for that food so long a time.
Didst thou but know the inly touch of love.

SCENE 12
*Exterior. Verona.*
*A Summer Evening.*
See note 13 (page 87).

Thou wouldst as soon go kindle fire with snow
As seek to quench the fire of love with words.                    20
LUC. I do not seek to quench your love's hot fire,
But qualify the fire's extreme rage,
Lest it should burn above the bounds of reason.
JUL. The more thou dam'st it up, the more it burns.
The current that with gentle murmur glides,                       25
Thou know'st, being stopp'd, impatiently doth rage;
But when his fair course is not hindered,
He makes sweet music with th' enamell'd stones,
Giving a gentle kiss to every sedge
He overtaketh in his pilgrimage;                                  30
And so by many winding nooks he strays,
With willing sport, to the wild ocean.
Then let me go, and hinder not my course.
I'll be as patient as a gentle stream,
And make a pastime of each weary step,                            35
Till the last step have brought me to my love;
And there I'll rest as, after much turmoil,
A blessed soul doth in Elysium.
LUC. But in what habit will you go along?
JUL. Not like a woman, for I would prevent                        40
The loose encounters of lascivious men;
Gentle Lucetta, fit me with such weeds
As may beseem some well-reputed page.
LUC. Why then, your ladyship must cut your hair.
JUL. No, girl; I'll knit it up in silken strings                  45
With twenty odd-conceited true-love knots—
To be fantastic may become a youth
Of greater time than I shall show to be.
LUC. What fashion, madam, shall I make your breeches?
JUL. That fits as well as ' Tell me, good my lord,                50
What compass will you wear your farthingale'.
Why ev'n what fashion thou best likes, Lucetta.
LUC. You must needs have them with a codpiece, madam.
JUL. Out, out, Lucetta, that will be ill-favour'd.
LUC. A round hose, madam, now's not worth a pin,                  55
Unless you have a codpiece to stick pins on.
JUL. Lucetta, as thou lov'st me, let me have
What thou think'st meet, and is most mannerly.
But tell me, wench, how will the world repute me
For undertaking so unstaid a journey?                             60
I fear me it will make me scandaliz'd.
LUC. If you think so, then stay at home and go not.
JUL. Nay, that I will not.
LUC. Then never dream on infamy, but go.
If Proteus like your journey when you come,                       65
No matter who's displeas'd when you are gone.
I fear me he will scarce be pleas'd withal.
JUL. That is the least, Lucetta, of my fear:
A thousand oaths, an ocean of his tears,
And instances of infinite of love,                               70
Warrant me welcome to my Proteus.
LUC. All these are servants to deceitful men.

JUL. Base men that use them to so base effect!
But truer stars did govern Proteus' birth;
His words are bonds, his oaths are oracles,                    75
His love sincere, his thoughts immaculate,
His tears pure messengers sent from his heart,
His heart as far from fraud as heaven from earth.
LUC. Pray heav'n he prove so when you come to him.
JUL. Now, as thou lov'st me, do him not that wrong           80
To bear a hard opinion of his truth :
Only deserve my love by loving him.
And presently go with me to my chamber,
To take a note of what I stand in need of
To furnish me upon my longing journey.                        85
All that is mine I leave at thy dispose,
My goods, my lands, my reputation ;
Only, in lieu thereof, dispatch me hence.
Come, answer not, but to it presently ;                       89
I am impatient of my tarriance.                    [exeunt.

## ACT THREE.

SCENE I.   *Milan.   The* DUKE'S *palace.*

*Enter* DUKE, THURIO, *and* PROTEUS.

DUKE. Sir Thurio, give us leave, I pray, awhile ;
We have some secrets to confer about.              [*exit* THURIO.
Now tell me, Proteus, what's your will with me ?
PRO. My gracious lord, that which I would discover
The law of friendship bids me to conceal;                      5
But, when I call to mind your gracious favours
Done to me, undeserving as I am,
My duty pricks me on to utter that
Which else no worldly good should draw from me.
Know, worthy prince, Sir Valentine, my friend,               10
This night intends to steal away your daughter ;
Myself am one made privy to the plot.
I know you have determin'd to bestow her
On Thurio, whom your gentle daughter hates ;
And should she thus be stol'n away from you,                 15
It would be much vexation to your age.
Thus, for my duty's sake, I rather chose
To cross my friend in his intended drift
Than, by concealing it, heap on your head
A pack of sorrows which would press you down,                20
Being unprevented, to your timeless grave.
DUKE. Proteus, I thank thee for thine honest care,
Which to requite, command me while I live.
This love of theirs myself have often seen,
Haply when they have judg'd me fast asleep,                   25
And oftentimes have purpos'd to forbid
Sir Valentine her company and my court ;
But, fearing lest my jealous aim might err
And so, unworthily, disgrace the man,
A rashness that I ever yet have shunn'd,                      30
I gave him gentle looks, thereby to find

SCENE 13
*Interior/Exterior.*
*Milan. The Duke's*
*Palace, with the Garden*
*of Love in the back-*
*ground. Day.*
DUKE, THURIO and
PROTEUS enter to
stately music.

60

That which thyself hast now disclos'd to me.
And, that thou mayst perceive my fear of this,
Knowing that tender youth is soon suggested,
I nightly lodge her in an upper tow'r,                    35
The key whereof myself have ever kept ;
And thence she cannot be convey'd away.
PRO. Know, noble lord, they have devis'd a mean
How he her chamber window will ascend
And with a corded ladder fetch her down ;                    40
For which the youthful lover now is gone,
And this way comes he with it presently ;
Where, if it please you, you may intercept him.
But, good my lord, do it so cunningly
That my discovery be not aimed at ;                    45
For love of you, not hate unto my friend,
Hath made me publisher of this pretence.
DUKE. Upon mine honour, he shall never know
That I had any light from thee of this.                    49
PRO. Adieu, my lord ; Sir Valentine is coming.          [exit.

*Enter* VALENTINE.

DUKE. Sir Valentine, whither away so fast ?
VAL. Please it your Grace, there is a messenger
That stays to bear my letters to my friends,
And I am going to deliver them.
DUKE. Be they of much import ?                    50
VAL. The tenour of them doth but signify
My health and happy being at your court.
DUKE. Nay then, no matter ; stay with me awhile ;
I am to break with thee of some affairs
That touch me near, wherein thou must be secret.                    60
'Tis not unknown to thee that I have sought
To match my friend Sir Thurio to my daughter.
VAL. I know it well, my lord ; and, sure, the match
Were rich and honourable ; besides, the gentleman
Is full of virtue, bounty, worth, and qualities                    65
Beseeming such a wife as your fair daughter.
Cannot your grace win her to fancy him ?
DUKE. No, trust me ; she is peevish, sullen, forward,
Proud, disobedient, stubborn, lacking duty ;
Neither regarding that she is my child                    70
Nor fearing me as if I were her father ;
And, may I say to thee, this pride of hers,
Upon advice, hath drawn my love from her ;
And, where I thought the remnant of mine age
Should have been cherish'd by her childlike duty,                    75
I now am full resolv'd to take a wife
And turn her out to who will take her in.
Then let her beauty be her wedding-dow'r ;
For me and my possessions she esteems not.
VAL. What would your Grace have me to do in this ?                    80
DUKE. There is a lady, in Verona here,
Whom I affect ; but she is nice, and coy,

| Line 34 omitted.

'the city' for 'Verona'.
See note 14 (page 87).

And nought esteems my aged eloquence.
Now, therefore, would I have thee to my tutor—
For long agone I have forgot to court ;                    85
Besides, the fashion of the time is chang'd-
How and which way I may bestow myself
To be regarded in her sun-bright eye.
VAL. Win her with gifts, if she respect not words:
Dumb jewels often in their silent kind                    90
More than quick words do move a woman's mind.
DUKE. But she did scorn a present that I sent her.
VAL. A woman sometime scorns what best contents her.
Send her another ; never give her o'er,
For scorn at first makes after-love the more.            95
If she do frown, 'tis not in hate of you,
But rather to beget more love in you ;
If she do chide, 'tis not to have you gone,
For why the fools are mad if left alone.
Take no repulse, whatever she doth say ;                 100
For ' Get you gone ' she doth not mean ' Away ! '
Flatter and praise, commend, extol their graces ;
Though ne'er so black, say they have angels' faces.
That man that hath a tongue, I say, is no man,
If with his tongue he cannot win a woman.               105
DUKE. But she I mean is promis'd by her friends
Unto a youthful gentleman of worth ;
And kept severely from resort of men,
That no man hath access by day to her.
VAL. Why then I would resort to her by night.          110
DUKE. Ay, but the doors be lock'd and keys kept safe,
That no man hath recourse to her by night.
VAL. What lets but one may enter at her window ?
DUKE. Her chamber is aloft, far from the ground,
And built so shelving that one cannot climb it          115
Without apparent hazard of his life.
VAL. Why then a ladder, quaintly made of cords,
To cast up with a pair of anchoring hooks,
Would serve to scale another Hero's tow'r,
So bold Leander would adventure it.                      120
DUKE. Now, as thou art a gentleman of blood,
Advise me where I may have such a ladder.
VAL. When would you use it ?  Pray, sir, tell me that.
DUKE. This very night ; for Love is like a child,
That longs for everything that he can come by.           125
VAL. By seven o'clock I'll get you such a ladder.
DUKE. But, hark thee ; I will go to her alone ;
How shall I best convey the ladder thither ?
VAL. It will be light, my lord, that you may bear it
Under a cloak that is of any length.                     130
DUKE. A cloak as long as thine will serve the turn ?
VAL. Ay, my good lord.
DUKE.                        Then let me see thy cloak.
I'll get me one of such another length.
VAL. Why, any cloak will serve the turn, my lord.
DUKE. How shall I fashion me to wear a cloak ?           135

Line 84 spoken after
line 86.

62

I pray thee, let me feel thy cloak upon me.
What letter is this same ?   What's here ?   ' To Silvia ' !
And here an engine fit for my proceeding !
I'll be so bold to break the seal for once.                    [*reads.*
  ' My thoughts do harbour with my Silvia nightly,            140
    And slaves they are to me, that send them flying.
  O, could their master come and go as lightly,
    Himself would lodge where, senseless, they are lying !
  My herald thoughts in thy pure bosom rest them,
    While I, their king, that thither them importune,         145
  Do curse the grace that with such grace hath blest them,
    Because myself do want my servants' fortune.
  I curse myself, for they are sent by me,
    That they should harbour where their lord should be.'
What's here ?                                                 150
  ' Silvia, this night I will enfranchise thee.'
'Tis so ; and here's the ladder for the purpose.
Why, Phaethon—for thou art Merops' son—
Wilt thou aspire to guide the heavenly car,
And with thy daring folly burn the world ?                    155
Wilt thou reach stars because they shine on thee ?
Go, base intruder, over-weening slave,
Bestow thy fawning smiles on equal mates ;
And think my patience, more than thy desert,
Is privilege for thy departure hence.                         160
Thank me for this more than for all the favours
Which, all too much, I have bestow'd on thee.
But if thou linger in my territories
Longer than swiftest expedition
Will give thee time to leave our royal court,                 165
By heaven ! my wrath shall far exceed the love
I ever bore my daughter or thyself.
Be gone ; I will not hear thy vain excuse,
But, as thou lov'st thy life, make speed from hence.  [*exit* DUKE.
VAL. And why not death rather than living torment ?           170
To die is to be banish'd from myself,
And Silvia is myself ; banish'd from her
Is self from self, a deadly banishment.
What light is light, if Silvia be not seen ?
What joy is joy, if Silvia be not by ?                        175
Unless it be to think that she is by,
And feed upon the shadow of perfection.
Except I be by Silvia in the night,
There is no music in the nightingale ;
Unless I look on Silvia in the day,                           180
There is no day for me to look upon.
She is my essence, and I leave to be
If I be not by her fair influence
Foster'd, illumin'd, cherish'd, kept alive.
I fly not death, to fly his deadly doom :                     185
Tarry I here, I but attend on death ;
But fly I hence, I fly away from life.

               *Enter* PROTEUS *and* LAUNCE.

BRO. Run, boy, run, run, and seek him out.
LAUN. So-ho, so-ho!
PRO. What seest thou? 190
LAUN. Him we go to find: there's not a hair on 's head but 'tis a
Valentine.
PRO. Valentine?
VAL. No.
PRO. Who then? his spirit? 195
VAL. Neither.
PRO. What then?
VAL. Nothing.
LAUN. Can nothing speak? Master, shall I strike?
PRO. Who wouldst thou strike? 200
LAUN. Nothing.
PRO. Villain, forbear.
LAUN. Why, sir, I'll strike nothing. I pray you—
PRO. Sirrah, I say, forbear. Friend Valentine, a word.
VAL. My ears are stopp'd and cannot hear good news, 205
So much of bad already hath possess'd them.
PRO. Then in dumb silence will I bury mine,
For they are harsh, untuneable, and bad.
VAL. Is Silvia dead?
PRO. No, Valentine. 210
VAL. No Valentine, indeed, for sacred Silvia.
Hath she forsworn me?
PRO. No, Valentine.
VAL. No Valentine, if Silvia have forsworn me.
What is your news? 215
LAUN. Sir, there is a proclamation that you are vanished.
PRO. That thou art banished—O, that's the news:—
From hence, from Silvia, and from me thy friend.
VAL. O, I have fed upon this woe already,
And now excess of it will make me surfeit. 220
Doth Silvia know that I am banished?
PRO. Ay, ay; and she hath offered to the doom—
Which, unrevers'd, stands in effectual force—
A sea of melting pearl, which some call tears;
Those at her father's churlish feet she tender'd: 225
With them, upon her knees, her humble self,
Wringing her hands, whose whiteness so became them
As if but now they waxed pale for woe.
But neither bended knees, pure hands held up,
Sad sighs, deep groans, nor silver-shedding tears, 230
Could penetrate her uncompassionate sire—
But Valentine, if he be ta'en, must die.
Besides, her intercession chaf'd him so,
When she for thy repeal was suppliant,
That to close prison he commanded her, 235
With many bitter threats of biding there.
VAL. No more; unless the next word that thou speak'st
Have some malignant power upon my life:
If so, I pray thee breathe it in mine ear,
As ending anthem of my endless dolour. 240
PRO. Cease to lament for that thou canst not help,

And study help for that which thou lament'st.
Time is the nurse and breeder of all good.
Here if thou stay thou canst not see thy love ;
Besides, thy staying will abridge thy life.                    245
Hope is a lover's staff ; walk hence with that,
And manage it against despairing thoughts.
Thy letters may be here, though thou art hence,
Which, being writ to me, shall be deliver'd
Even in the milk-white bosom of thy love.                      250
The time now serves not to expostulate.
Come, I'll convey thee through the city gate ;
And, ere I part with thee, confer at large
Of all that may concern thy love affairs.
As thou lov'st Silvia, though not for thyself,                 255
Regard thy danger, and along with me.
VAL. I pray thee, Launce, an if thou seest my boy,
Bid him make haste and meet me at the Northgate.
PRO. Go, sirrah, find him out. Come, Valentine.
VAL. O my dear Silvia ! Hapless Valentine !                    260
                    [*exeunt* VALENTINE *and* PROTEUS.
LAUN. I am but a fool, look you, and yet I have the wit to
think my master is a kind of a knave ; but that's all one if he
be but one knave. He lives not now that knows me to be
in love ; yet I am in love ; but a team of horse shall not pluck
that from me ; nor who 'tis I love ; and yet 'tis a woman ; but
what woman I will not tell myself ; and yet 'tis a milkmaid ; yet
'tis not a maid, for she hath had gossips ; yet 'tis a maid, for she is
her master's maid and serves for wages. She hath more qualities
than a water-spaniel—which is much in a bare Christian. Here
is the cate-log [*pulling out a paper*] of her condition. ' Inprimis :    LAUNCE moves from
She can fetch and carry.' Why, a horse can do no more ; nay,     the Duke's palace area
a horse cannot fetch, but only carry ; therefore is she better than  to sit on a fountain by
a jade. ' Item : She can milk.' Look you, a sweet virtue in a    the arch.
maid with clean hands.                                          275

                          *Enter* SPEED.

SPEED. How now, Signior Launce ! What news with your master-
ship ?
LAUN. With my master's ship ? Why, it is at sea.
SPEED. Well, your old vice still : mistake the word. What news, then,
in your paper ?                                                280
LAUN. The black'st news that ever thou heard'st.
SPEED. Why, man ? how black ?
LAUN. Why, as black as ink.
SPEED. Let me read them.
LAUN. Fie on thee, jolt-head ; thou canst not read.            285
SPEED. Thou liest ; I can.
LAUN. I will try thee. Tell me this : Who begot thee ?
SPEED. Marry, the son of my grandfather.
LAUN. O illiterate loiterer. It was the son of thy grandmother. This
proves that thou canst not read.                               290
SPEED. Come, fool, come ; try me in thy paper.
LAUN. [*handing over the paper*.] There ; and Saint Nicholas be thy
speed.

SPEED. [*reads.*] ' Inprimis : She can milk.'
LAUN. Ay, that she can.
SPEED. ' Item : She brews good ale.' 295
LAUN. And thereof comes the proverb : Blessing of your heart, you brew good ale.
SPEED. ' Item : She can sew.'
LAUN. That's as much as to say ' Can she so ? '
SPEED. ' Item : She can knit.' 300
LAUN. What need a man care for a stock with a wench, when she can knit him a stock.
SPEED. ' Item : She can wash and scour.'
LAUN. A special virtue ; for then she need not be wash'd and scour'd.
SPEED. ' Item : She can spin.' 306
LAUN. Then may I set the world on wheels, when she can spin for her living.
SPEED. ' Item : She hath many nameless virtues.'
LAUN. That's as much as to say ' bastard virtues ' ; that indeed know not their fathers, and therefore have no names. 312
SPEED. ' Here follow her vices.'
LAUN. Close at the heels of her virtues.
SPEED. ' Item : She is not to be kiss'd fasting, in respect of her breath.'
LAUN. Well, that fault may be mended with a breakfast. Read on.
SPEED. ' Item : She hath a sweet mouth.'
LAUN. That makes amends for her sour breath. 320
SPEED. ' Item : She doth talk in her sleep.'
LAUN. It's no matter for that, so she sleep not in her talk.
SPEED. ' Item : She is slow in words.'
LAUN. O villain, that set this down among her vices ! To be slow in words is a woman's only virtue. I pray thee, out with't ; and place it for her chief virtue.
SPEED. ' Item : She is proud.'
LAUN. Out with that too ; it was Eve's legacy, and cannot be ta'en from her. 330
SPEED. ' Item : She hath no teeth.'
LAUN. I care not for that neither, because I love crusts.
SPEED. ' Item : She is curst.'
LAUN. Well, the best is, she hath no teeth to bite. 335
SPEED. ' Item : She will often praise her liquor.'
LAUN. If her liquor be good, she shall ; if she will not, I will ; for good things should be praised.
SPEED. ' Item : She is too liberal.' 339
LAUN. Of her tongue she cannot, for that's writ down she is slow of ; of her purse she shall not, for that I'll keep shut. Now of another thing she may, and that cannot I help. Well, proceed.
SPEED. ' Item : She hath more hair than wit, and more faults than hairs, and more wealth than faults.' 345
LAUN. Stop there ; I'll have her ; she was mine, and not mine, twice or thrice in that last article. Rehearse that once more.
SPEED. ' Item : She hath more hair than wit '— 349
LAUN. More hair than wit. It may be ; I'll prove it : the cover of the salt hides the salt, and therefore it is more than the salt ; the hair that covers the wit is more than the wit, for the greater hides the less. What's next ?

SPEED. ' And more faults than hairs '—
LAUN. That's monstrous. O that that were out !                    355
SPEED. ' And more wealth than faults.'
LAUN. Why, that word makes the faults gracious. Well, I'll have
    her ; an if it be a match, as nothing is impossible—
SPEED. What then ?                                               360
LAUN. Why, then will I tell thee—that thy master stays for thee at the
    Northgate.
SPEED. For me ?
LAUN. For thee ! ay, who art thou ?   He hath stay'd for a better man
    than thee.                                                   365
SPEED. And must I go to him ?
LAUN. Thou must run to him, for thou hast stay'd so long that going
    will scarce serve the turn.
SPEED. Why didst not tell me sooner ?   Pox of your love letters ! 370
                                                              [exit.
LAUN. Now will he be swing'd for reading my letter.   An unmannerly
    slave that will thrust himself into secrets !   I'll after, to rejoice in
    the boy's correction.                                    [exit.

> SCENE II.   *Milan.   The* DUKE'S *palace.*
> *Enter* DUKE *and* THURIO.

DUKE. Sir Thurio, fear not but that she will love you
    Now Valentine is banish'd from her sight.
THU. Since his exile she hath despis'd me most,
    Forsworn my company and rail'd at me,
    That I am desperate of obtaining her.                         5
DUKE. This weak impress of love is as a figure
    Trenched in ice, which with an hour's heat
    Dissolves to water and doth lose his form.
    A little time will melt her frozen thoughts,
    And worthless Valentine shall be forgot.                     10

> *Enter* PROTEUS.

    How now, Sir Proteus !   Is your countryman,
    According to our proclamation, gone ?
PRO. Gone, my good lord.
DUKE. My daughter takes his going grievously.
PRO. A little time, my lord, will kill that grief.               15
DUKE. So I believe ; but Thurio thinks not so.
    Proteus, the good conceit I hold of thee—
    For thou hast shown some sign of good desert—
    Makes me the better to confer with thee.
PRO. Longer than I prove loyal to your Grace                     20
    Let me not live to look upon your Grace.
DUKE. Thou know'st how willingly I would effect
    The match between Sir Thurio and my daughter.
PRO. I do, my lord.
DUKE. And also, I think, thou art not ignorant                   25
    How she opposes her against my will.
PRO. She did, my lord, when Valentine was here.
DUKE. Ay, and perversely she persevers so.
    What might we do to make the girl forget
    The love of Valentine, and love Sir Thurio ?                 30

SCENE 14
*Interior/Exterior.*
*Milan. The Duke's*
*Palace, with the Garden*
*of Love in the back-*
*ground. Day.*

PRO. The best way is to slander Valentine
    With falsehood, cowardice, and poor descent—
    Three things that women highly hold in hate.
DU E. Ay, but she'll think that it is spoke in hate.
PR . Ay, if his enemy deliver it ;                      35
    Therefore it must with circumstance be spoken
    By one whom she esteemeth as his friend.
DUKE. Then you must undertake to slander him.
PRO. And that, my lord, I shall be loath to do :
    'Tis an ill office for a gentleman,                 40
    Especially against his very friend.
DUKE. Where your good word cannot advantage him,
    Your slander never can endamage him ;
    Therefore the office is indifferent,
    Being entreated to it by your friend.            45
PRO. You have prevail'd, my lord ; if I can do it
    By aught that I can speak in his dispraise,
    She shall not long continue love to him.
    But say this weed her love from Valentine,     'wind' for 'weed'.
    It follows not that she will love Sir Thurio.    50   See note 15 (page 87).
THU. Therefore, as you unwind her love from him,
    Lest it should ravel and be good to none,
    You must provide to bottom it on me ;
    Which must be done by praising me as much
    As you in worth dispraise Sir Valentine.       55
DUKE. And, Proteus, we dare trust you in this kind,
    Because we know, on Valentine's report,
    You are already Love's firm votary
    And cannot soon revolt and change your mind.
    Upon this warrant shall you have access       60
    Where you with Silvia may confer at large—
    For she is lumpish, heavy, melancholy,
    And, for your friend's sake, will be glad of you—
    Where you may temper her by your persuasion
    To hate young Valentine and love my friend.    65
PRO. As much as I can do I will effect.
    But you, Sir Thurio, are not sharp enough ;
    You must lay lime to tangle her desires
    By wailful sonnets, whose composed rhymes
    Should be full-fraught with serviceable vows.    70
DUKE. Ay,
    Much is the force of heaven-bred poesy.
PRO. Say that upon the altar of her beauty
    You sacrifice your tears, your sighs, your heart ;
    Write till your ink be dry, and with your tears    75
    Moist it again, and frame some feeling line
    That may discover such integrity ;
    For Orpheus' lute was strung with poets' sinews.
    Whose golden touch could soften steel and stones,
    Make tigers tame, and huge leviathans       80
    Forsake unsounded deeps to dance on sands.
    After your dire-lamenting elegies,
    Visit by night your lady's chamber window

With some sweet consort; to their instruments
Tune a deploring dump—the night's dead silence          85
Will well become such sweet-complaining grievance.
This, or else nothing, will inherit her.
DUKE. This discipline shows thou hast been in love.
THU. And thy advice this night I'll put in practice;
Therefore, sweet Proteus, my direction-giver,          90
Let us into the city presently
To sort some gentlemen well skill'd in music.
I have a sonnet that will serve the turn
To give the onset to thy good advice.
DUKE. About it, gentlemen!                              95
PRO. We'll wait upon your Grace till after supper,
And afterward determine our proceedings.
DUKE. Even now about it! I will pardon you.            [*exeunt.*

ACT FOUR.

SCENE I.    *The frontiers of Mantua.    A forest.*

*Enter certain* OUTLAWS.

1 OUT. Fellows, stand fast; I see a passenger.
2 OUT. If there be ten, shrink not, but down with 'em.

*Enter* VALENTINE *and* SPEED.

3 OUT. Stand, sir, and throw us that you have about ye;
If not, we'll make you sit, and rifle you.
SPEED. Sir, we are undone; these are the villains        5
That all the travellers do fear so much.
VAL. My friends—
1 OUT. That's not so, sir; we are your enemies.
2 OUT. Peace! we'll hear him.
3 OUT. Ay, by my beard, will we; for he is a proper man. 10
VAL. Then know that I have little wealth to lose;
A man I am cross'd with adversity;
My riches are these poor habiliments,
Of which if you should here disfurnish me,
You take the sum and substance that I have.             15
2 OUT. Whither travel you?
VAL. To Verona.
1 OUT. Whence came you?
VAL. From Milan.
3 OUT. Have you long sojourn'd there?                    20
VAL. Some sixteen months, and longer might have stay'd,
If crooked fortune had not thwarted me.
1 OUT. What, were you banish'd thence?
VAL. I was.
2 OUT. For what offence?                                 25
VAL. For that which now torments me to rehearse:
I kill'd a man, whose death I much repent;
But yet I slew him manfully in fight,
Without false vantage or base treachery.
1 OUT. Why, ne'er repent it, if it were done so.         30
But were you banish'd for so small a fault?
VAL. I was, and held me glad of such a doom.

SCENE 15
*Exterior. A shadowy
Forest. Day.*
See note 16 (page 88).

2 OUT. Have you the tongues?
VAL. My youthful travel therein made me happy,
  Or else I often had been miserable.                                            35
3 OUT. By the bare scalp of Robin Hood's fat friar,
  This fellow were a king for our wild faction!
1 OUT. We'll have him. Sirs, a word.
SPEED. Master, be one of them; it's an honourable kind of thievery.
VAL. Peace, villain!                                                                      41
2 OUT. Tell us this: have you anything to take to?
VAL. Nothing but my fortune.
3 OUT. Know, then, that some of us are gentlemen,
  Such as the fury of ungovern'd youth                                          45
  Thrust from the company of awful men;
  Myself was from Verona banished
  For practising to steal away a lady,
  An heir, and near allied unto the Duke.
2 OUT. And I from Mantua, for a gentleman                                       50
  Who, in my mood, I stabb'd unto the heart.
1 OUT. And I for such-like petty crimes as these.
  But to the purpose—for we cite our faults
  That they may hold excus'd our lawless lives;
  And, partly, seeing you are beautified                                       55
  With goodly shape, and by your own report
  A linguist, and a man of such perfection
  As we do in our quality much want—
2 OUT. Indeed, because you are a banish'd man,
  Therefore, above the rest, we parley to you.                                 60
  Are you content to be our general—
  To make a virtue of necessity,
  And live as we do in this wilderness?
3 OUT. What say'st thou? Wilt thou be of our consort?
  Say 'ay' and be the captain of us all.                                        65
  We'll do thee homage, and be rul'd by thee,
  Love thee as our commander and our king.
1 OUT. But if thou scorn our courtesy thou diest.
2 OUT. Thou shalt not live to brag what we have offer'd.
VAL. I take your offer, and will live with you,                                  70
  Provided that you do no outrages
  On silly women or poor passengers.
3 OUT. No, we detest such vile base practices.
  Come, go with us; we'll bring thee to our crews,
  And show thee all the treasure we have got;                                  75
  Which, with ourselves, all rest at thy dispose.          [exeunt.

SCENE II.  *Milan.  Outside the* DUKE'S *palace, under* SILVIA'S *window.*

*Enter* PROTEUS.

PRO. Already have I been false to Valentine,
  And now I must be as unjust to Thurio.
  Under the colour of commending him
  I have access my own love to prefer;
  But Silvia is too fair, too true, too holy,                                   5
  To be corrupted with my worthless gifts.
  When I protest true loyalty to her,

---

'Sirs, a word' spoken
by 3 OUTLAW.

---

SCENE 16
*Exterior. Milan.
Outside Silvia's Tower.
Night. Moonrise.*

She twits me with my falsehood to my friend ;
When to her beauty I commend my vows,
She bids me think how I have been forsworn                    10
In breaking faith with Julia whom I lov'd ;
And notwithstanding all her sudden quips,
The least whereof would quell a lover's hope,
Yet, spaniel-like, the more she spurns my love
The more it grows and fawneth on her still.                   15

                    *Enter* THURIO *and* MUSICIANS.                     See note 17 (page 88).

But here comes Thurio. Now must we to her window,
And give some evening music to her ear.
THU. How now, Sir Proteus, are you crept before us ?
PRO. Ay, gentle Thurio ; for you know that love
    Will creep in service where it cannot go.                 20
THU. Ay, but I hope, sir, that you love not here.
PRO. Sir, but I do ; or else I would be hence.
THU. Who ?  Silvia?
PRO.                       Ay, Silvia—for your sake.
THU. I thank you for your own.  Now, gentlemen,
    Let's tune, and to it lustily awhile.                     25

        *Enter at a distance,* HOST, *and* JULIA *in boy's clothes.*      See note 18 (page 88).

HOST. Now, my young guest, methinks you're allycholly ; I pray you,
    why is it ?
JUL. Marry, mine host, because I cannot be merry.
HOST. Come, we'll have you merry ; I'll bring you where you shall
    hear music, and see the gentleman that you ask'd for.     31
JUL. But shall I hear him speak ?
HOST. Ay, that you shall.                          [*music plays.*
JUL. That will be music.
HOST. Hark, hark !                                               35
JUL. Is he among these ?
HOST. Ay ; but peace ! let's hear 'em.

                        *Song.*                               See note 19 (page 88).

        Who is Silvia ?  What is she,
            That all our swains commend her ?
        Holy, fair, and wise is she ;
            The heaven such grace did lend her,           40
        That she might admired be.

        Is she kind as she is fair ?
            For beauty lives with kindness.
        Love doth to her eyes repair,                       45
            To help him of his blindness ;
        And, being help'd, inhabits there.

        Then to Silvia let us sing
            That Silvia is excelling ;                      50
        She excels each mortal thing
            Upon the dull earth dwelling.
        To her let us garlands bring.

*Tyler Butterworth as Proteus*

HOST. How now, are you sadder than you were before ? How do you,
    man ?   The music likes you not.
JUL. You mistake ;  the musician likes me not.                    55
HOST. Why, my pretty youth ?
JUL. He plays false, father.
HOST. How, out of tune on the strings ?
JUL. Not so ;  but yet so false that he grieves my very heart-strings.
HOST. You have a quick ear.                                       61
JUL. Ay, I would I were deaf ; it makes me have a slow heart.
HOST. I perceive you delight not in music.
JUL. Not a whit, when it jars so.                                 65
HOST. Hark, what fine change is in the music !
JUL. Ay, that change is the spite.
HOST. You would have them always play but one thing ?
JUL. I would always have one play but one thing.
    But, Host, doth this Sir Proteus, that we talk on,            70
    Often resort unto this gentlewoman ?
HOST. I tell you what Launce, his man, told me : he lov'd her out of
    all nick.
JUL. Where is Launce ?                                            74
HOST. Gone to seek his dog, which to-morrow, by his master's com-
    mand, he must carry for a present to his lady.
JUL. Peace, stand aside ;  the company parts.
PRO. Sir Thurio, fear not you ;  I will so plead
    That you shall say my cunning drift excels.
THU. Where meet we ?
PRO.                         At Saint Gregory's well.
THU.                                         Farewell.            80
                     [*exeunt* THURIO *and* MUSICIANS.

      *Enter* SILVIA *above, at her window.*

PRO. Madam, good ev'n to your ladyship.
SIL. I thank you for your music, gentlemen.
    Who is that that spake ?
PRO. One, lady, if you knew his pure heart's truth,
    You would quickly learn to know him by his voice.            85
SIL. Sir Proteus, as I take it.
PRO. Sir Proteus, gentle lady, and your servant.
SIL. What's your will ?
PRO.                         That I may compass yours.
SIL.. You have your wish ;  my will is even this,
    That presently you hie you home to bed.                      90
    Thou subtle, perjur'd, false, disloyal man,
    Think'st thou I am so shallow, so conceitless,
    To be seduced by thy flattery
    That hast deceiv'd so many with thy vows ?
    Return, return, and make thy love amends.                    95
    For me, by this pale queen of night I swear,
    I am so far from granting thy request
    That I despise thee for thy wrongful suit,
    And by and by intend to chide myself
    Even for this time I spend in talking to thee.               100
PRO. I grant, sweet love, that I did love a lady ;
    But she is dead.

JUL. [*aside*.] 'Twere false, if I should speak it ;
    For I am sure she is not buried.
SIL. Say that she be ; yet Valentine, thy friend,
    Survives, to whom, thyself art witness,           105
    I am betroth'd ; and art thou not asham'd
    To wrong him with thy importunacy ?
PRO. I likewise hear that Valentine is dead.
SIL. And so suppose am I ; for in his grave
    Assure thyself my love is buried.             110
PRO. Sweet lady, let me rake it from the earth.
SIL. Go to thy lady's grave, and call hers thence ;
    Or, at the least, in hers sepulchre thine.
JUL. [*aside*.] He heard not that.
PRO. Madam, if your heart be so obdurate,        115
    Vouchsafe me yet your picture for my love,
    The picture that is hanging in your chamber ;
    To that I'll speak, to that I'll sigh and weep ;
    For, since the substance of your perfect self
    Is else devoted, I am but a shadow ;        120
    And to your shadow will I make true love.
JUL. [*aside*.] If 'twere a substance, you would, sure, deceive it
    And make it but a shadow, as I am.
SIL. I am very loath to be your idol, sir ;
    But since your falsehood shall become you well    125
    To worship shadows and adore false shapes,
    Send to me in the morning, and I'll send it .
    And so, good rest.
PRO.               As wretches have o'ernight
    That wait for execution in the morn.
                    [*exeunt* PROTEUS *and* SILVIA.
JUL. Host, will you go ?               130
HOST. By my halidom, I was fast asleep.
JUL. Pray you, where lies Sir Proteus ?
HOST. Marry, at my house. Trust me, I think 'tis almost day.
JUL. Not so ; but it hath been the longest night    135
    That e'er I watch'd, and the most heaviest.
                           [*exeunt*.

SCENE III.    *Under* SILVIA's *window*.

*Enter* EGLAMOUR.

EGL. This is the hour that Madam Silvia
    Entreated me to call and know her mind ;
    There's some great matter she'd employ me in.
    Madam, madam !

*Enter* SILVIA *above, at her window*.

SIL.               Who calls ?
EGL.                   Your servant and your friend ;
    One that attends your ladyship's command.    5
SIL. Sir Eglamour, a thousand times good morrow !
EGL. As many, worthy lady, to yourself !
    According to your ladyship's impose,
    I am thus early come to know what service
    It is your pleasure to command me in.       10

SCENE 17
*Exterior. Milan.*
*Outside Silvia's Tower*
*and in the Garden of*
*Love. Dawn.*
SILVIA comes out of her
Tower and walks
through heavy ground
mist to the Garden of
Love, where SIR
EGLAMOUR is waiting
for her.

SIL. O Eglamour, thou art a gentleman—
    Think not I flatter, for I swear I do not—
    Valiant, wise, remorseful, well accomplish'd.
    Thou art not ignorant what dear good will
    I bear unto the banish'd Valentine ;                                    15
    Nor how my father would enforce me marry
    Vain Thurio, whom my very soul abhors.
    Thyself hast lov'd ; and I have heard thee say
    No grief did ever come so near thy heart
    As when thy lady and thy true love died,                                20
    Upon whose grave thou vow'dst pure chastity.
    Sir Eglamour, I would to Valentine,
    To Mantua, where I hear he makes abode ;
    And, for the ways are dangerous to pass,
    I do desire thy worthy company,                                         25
    Upon whose faith and honour I repose.
    Urge not my father's anger, Eglamour,
    But think upon my grief, a lady's grief,.
    And on the justice of my flying hence
    To keep me from a most unholy match,                                    30
    Which heaven and fortune still rewards with plagues.
    I do desire thee, even from a heart
    As full of sorrows as the sea of sands,
    To bear me company and go with me ;
    If not, to hide what I have said to thee,                               35
    That I may venture to depart alone.
EGL. Madam, I pity much your grievances ;
    Which since I know they virtuously are plac'd,
    I give consent to go along with you,
    Recking as little what betideth me                                      40
    As much I wish all good befortune you.
    When will you go ?
SIL.                                     This evening coming.
EGL. Where shall I meet you ?
SIL.                                     At Friar Patrick's cell,
    Where I intend holy confession.
EGL. I will not fail your ladyship.  Good morrow, gentle lady.  46
SIL. Good morrow, kind Sir Eglamour.                          [exeunt.

SCENE IV.  Under SILVIA's *window*.

*Enter* LAUNCE, *with his dog.*

LAUN. When a man's servant shall play the cur with him, look you,
it goes hard—one that I brought up of a puppy ; one that I sav'd
from drowning, when three or four of his blind brothers and sisters
went to it.  I have taught him, even as one would say precisely
'Thus I would teach a dog'.  I was sent to deliver him as a
present to Mistress Silvia from my master ; and I came no sooner
into the dining-chamber, but he steps me to her trencher and
steals her capon's leg.  O, 'tis a foul thing when a cur cannot
keep himself in all companies !  I would have, as one should say,
one that takes upon him to be a dog indeed, to be, as it were, a dog
at all things.  If I had not had more wit than he, to take a fault
upon me that he did, I think verily he had been hang'd for't ;

SCENE 18
*Exterior. Milan. By an
arch near Silvia's
Tower. Early Evening.*

sure as I live, he had suffer'd for't.  You shall judge.  He thrusts
me himself into the company of three or four gentleman-like dogs
under the Duke's table ;  he had not been there, bless the mark, a
pissing while but all the chamber smelt him.   ' Out with the dog '
says one ;  ' What cur is that ? ' says another ;  ' Whip him out '
says the third ;  ' Hang him up ' says the Duke.   I, having been
acquainted with the smell before, knew it was Crab, and goes me
to the fellow that whips the dogs.   ' Friend,' quoth I ' you mean
to whip the dog.'   ' Ay, marry do I ' quoth he.   ' You do him
the more wrong ; ' quoth I ' 'twas I did the thing you wot of.'
He makes me no more ado, but whips me out of the chamber.
How many masters would do this for his servant ?   Nay, I'll be
sworn, I have sat in the stock for puddings he hath stol'n, otherwise
he had been executed ;  I have stood on the pillory for geese he
hath kill'd, otherwise he had suffer'd for't.   Thou think'st not
of this now.   Nay, I remember the trick you serv'd me when I
took my leave of Madam Silvia.   Did not I bid thee still mark me
and do as I do ?   When didst thou see me heave up my leg and
make water against a gentlewoman's farthingale ?   Didst thou
ever see me do such a trick ?                                36

*Enter* PROTEUS *and* JULIA *in boy's clothes.*

PRO. Sebastian is thy name ?   I like thee well,
And will employ thee in some service presently.
JUL. In what you please ;  I'll do what I can.
PRO. I hope thou wilt.  [*to Launce.*]  How now, you whoreson
peasant !                                                   40
Where have you been these two days loitering ?
LAUN. Marry, sir, I carried Mistress Silvia the dog you bade me.
PRO. And what says she to my little jewel ?
LAUN. Marry, she says your dog was a cur, and tells you currish
thanks is good enough for such a present.                   46
PRO. But she receiv'd my dog ?
LAUN. No, indeed, did she not ;  here have I brought him back again.
PRO. What, didst thou offer her this from me ?              50
LAUN. Ay, sir ;  the other squirrel was stol'n from me by the hang-
man's boys in the market-place ;  and then I offer'd her mine own,
who is a dog as big as ten of yours, and therefore the gift the
greater.
PRO. Go, get thee hence and find my dog again,             55
Or ne'er return again into my sight.
Away, I say.   Stayest thou to vex me here ?

[*exit* LAUNCE.

A slave that still an end turns me to shame !
Sebastian, I have entertained thee
Partly that I have need of such a youth
That can with some discretion do my business,
For 'tis no trusting to yond foolish lout,
But chiefly for thy face and thy behaviour,
Which, if my augury deceive me not,
Witness good bringing up, fortune, and truth ;             65
Therefore, know thou, for this I entertain thee.
Go presently, and take this ring with thee,
Deliver it to Madam Silvia—

SCENE 19
*Exterior. Milan. In a
small courtyard outside
the Garden of Love, by
the arch leading to
Silvia's Tower. Early
Evening.*

She lov'd me well deliver'd it to me.
JUL. It seems you lov'd not her, to leave her token.          70
She is dead, belike?
PRO.                    Not so; I think she lives.
JUL. Alas!
PRO. Why dost thou cry ' Alas '?
JUL.                    I cannot choose
But pity her.
PRO. Wherefore shouldst thou pity her?
JUL. Because methinks that she lov'd you as well          75
As you do love your lady Silvia.
She dreams on him that has forgot her love :
You dote on her that cares nor for your love.
'Tis pity love should be so contrary;
And thinking on it makes me cry ' Alas ! '          80
PRO. Well, give her that ring, and therewithal
This letter. That's her chamber. Tell my lady
I claim the promise for her heavenly picture.
Your message done, hie home unto my chamber,
Where thou shalt find me sad and solitary.          [exit PROTEUS.
JUL. How many women would do such a message?          86
Alas, poor Proteus, thou hast entertain'd
A fox to be the shepherd of thy lambs.
Alas, poor fool, why do I pity him
That with his very heart despiseth me?          90
Because he loves her, he despiseth me;
Because I love him, I must pity him.
This ring I gave him, when he parted from me,
To bind him to remember my good will;
And now am I, unhappy messenger,          95
To plead for that which I would not obtain,
To carry that which I would have refus'd,
To praise his faith, which I would have disprais'd.
I am my master's true confirmed love,
But cannot be true servant to my master          100
Unless I prove false traitor to myself.
Yet will I woo for him, but yet so coldly
As, heaven it knows, I would not have him speed.

            *Enter* SILVIA, *attended.*                    See note 20 (page 88).

Gentlewoman, good day! I pray you be my mean
To bring me where to speak with Madam Silvia.          105
SIL. What would you with her, if that I be she?
JUL. If you be she, I do entreat your patience
To hear me speak the message I am sent on.
SIL. From whom?
JUL. From my master, Sir Proteus, madam.          110
SIL. O, he sends you for a picture?
JUL. Ay, madam.
SIL. Ursula, bring my picture there.
Go, give your master this. Tell him from me,
One Julia, that his changing thoughts forget,          115
Would better fit his chamber than this shadow.
JUL. Madam, please you peruse this letter.

Pardon me, madam ; I have unadvis'd
Deliver'd you a paper that I should not.
This is the letter to your ladyship.                    120
SIL. I pray thee let me look on that again.
JUL. It may not be ; good madam, pardon me.
SIL. There, hold !
    I will not look upon your master's lines.
    I know they are stuff'd with protestations,        125
    And full of new-found oaths, which he will break
    As easily as I do tear his paper.
JUL. Madam, he sends your ladyship this ring.
SIL. The more shame for him that he sends it me ;
    For I have heard him say a thousand times           130
    His Julia gave it him at his departure.
    Though his false finger have profan'd the ring,
    Mine shall not do his Julia so much wrong.
JUL. She thanks you.
SIL. What say'st thou ?                                 135
JUL. I thank you, madam, that you tender her.
    Poor gentlewoman, my master wrongs her much.
SIL. Dost thou know her ?
JUL. Almost as well as I do know myself.
    To think upon her woes, I do protest               140
    That I have wept a hundred several times.
SIL. Belike she thinks that Proteus hath forsook her.
JUL. I think she doth, and that's her cause of sorrow.
SIL. Is she not passing fair ?
JUL. She hath been fairer, madam, than she is.         145
    When she did think my master lov'd her well,
    She, in my judgment, was as fair as you ;
    But since she did neglect her looking-glass
    And threw her sun-expelling mask away,
    The air hath starv'd the roses in her cheeks       150
    And pinch'd the lily-tincture of her face,
    That now she is become as black as I.
SIL. How tall was she ?
JUL. About my stature ; for at Pentecost,
    When all our pageants of delight were play'd,       155
    Our youth got me to play the woman's part,
    And I was trimm'd in Madam Julia's gown ;
    Which served me as fit, by all men's judgments,
    As if the garment had been made for me ;
    Therefore I know she is about my height.            160
    And at that time I made her weep agood,
    For I did play a lamentable part.
    Madam, 'twas Ariadne passioning
    For Theseus' perjury and unjust flight ;
    Which I so lively acted with my tears               165
    That my poor mistress, moved therewithal,
    Wept bitterly ; and would I might be dead
    If I in thought felt not her very sorrow.
SIL. She is beholding to thee, gentle youth.
    Alas, poor lady, desolate and left !                170
    I weep myself, to think upon thy words.

Here, youth, there is my purse ; I give thee this
For thy sweet mistress' sake, because thou lov'st her.
Farewell.                    [*exit* SILVIA *with attendants.*
JUL. And she shall thank you for't, if e'er you know her.    175
A virtuous gentlewoman, mild and beautiful !
I hope my master's suit will be but cold,
Since she respects my mistress' love so much.
Alas, how love can trifle with itself !
Here is her picture ; let me see.   I think,              180
If I had such a tire, this face of mine
Were full as lovely as is this of hers ;
And yet the painter flatter'd her a little,
Unless I flatter with myself too much.
Her hair is auburn, mine is perfect yellow ;            185
If that be all the difference in his love,
I'll get me such a colour'd periwig.
Her eyes are grey as glass, and so are mine ;          Line 188 omitted.
Ay, but her forehead's low, and mine's as high.        See note 21 (page 88).
What should it be that he respects in her              190
But I can make respective in myself,
If this fond Love were not a blinded god ?
Come, shadow, come, and take this shadow up,
For 'tis thy rival.   O thou senseless form,
Thou shalt be worshipp'd, kiss'd, lov'd, and ador'd !    195
And were there sense in his idolatry
My substance should be statue in thy stead.
I'll use thee kindly for thy mistress' sake,
That us'd me so ; or else, by Jove I vow,
I should have scratch'd out your unseeing eyes,        200
To make my master out of love with thee.               [*exit.*    JULIA goes away sadly
                                                                    through the Garden of
                                                                    Love.
### ACT FIVE.

SCENE I.   *Milan.   An abbey.*                         SCENE 20
                                                        *Exterior. Milan.*
*Enter* EGLAMOUR.                                       *Outside Friar Patrick's*
                                                        *Cell. Evening.*
EGL. The sun begins to gild the western sky,
And now it is about the very hour
That Silvia at Friar Patrick's cell should meet me.
She will not fail, for lovers break not hours
Unless it be to come before their time,                5
So much they spur their expedition.

*Enter* SILVIA.

See where she comes.   Lady, a happy evening !
SIL. Amen, amen !   Go on, good Eglamour,
Out at the postern by the abbey wall ;
I fear I am attended by some spies.                    10
EGL. Fear not.   The forest is not three leagues off ;
If we recover that, we are sure enough.                [*exeunt.*

SCENE II.   *Milan.   The* DUKE'S *palace.*             SCENE 21
                                                        *Exterior. Milan. The*
*Enter* THURIO, PROTEUS, *and* JULIA *as* SEBASTIAN.   *Garden of Love.*
                                                        *Evening.*
                                                        See note 22 (page 88).

THU. Sir Proteus, what says Silvia to my suit?
PRO. O, sir, I find her milder than she was;
  And yet she takes exceptions at your person.
THU. What, that my leg is too long?
PRO. No; that it is too little.                                   5
THU. I'll wear a boot to make it somewhat rounder.
JUL. [aside.] But love will not be spurr'd to what it loathes.
THU. What says she to my face?
PRO. She says it is a fair one.
THU. Nay, then, the wanton lies; my face is black.               10
PRO. But pearls are fair; and the old saying is:
  Black men are pearls in beauteous ladies' eyes.
JUL. [aside.] 'Tis true, such pearls as put out ladies' eyes;
  For I had rather wink than look on them.
THU. How likes she my discourse?                                 15
PRO. Ill, when you talk of war.
THU. But well when I discourse of love and peace?
JUL. [aside.] But better, indeed, when you hold your peace.
THU. What says she to my valour?
PRO. O, sir, she makes no doubt of that.                         20
JUL. [aside.] She needs not, when she knows it cowardice.
THU. What says she to my birth?
PRO. That you are well deriv'd.
JUL. [aside.] True; from a gentleman to a fool.
THU. Considers she my possessions?                               25
PRO. O, ay; and pities them.
THU. Wherefore?
JUL. [aside.] That such an ass should owe them.
PRO. That they are out by lease.
JUL. Here comes the Duke.                                        30

                    *Enter* DUKE.

DUKE. How now, Sir Proteus! how now, Thurio!
  Which of you saw Sir Eglamour of late?
THU. Not I.
PRO.          Nor I.
DUKE.                Saw you my daughter?
PRO.                                      Neither.
DUKE. Why then,
  She's fled unto that peasant Valentine;                        35
  And Eglamour is in her company.
  'Tis true; for Friar Lawrence met them both
  As he in penance wander'd through the forest;
  Him he knew well, and guess'd that it was she,
  But, being mask'd, he was not sure of it;                      40
  Besides, she did intend confession                   See note 23 (page 89).
  At Patrick's cell this even; and there she was not.
  These likelihoods confirm her flight from hence;
  Therefore, I pray you, stand not to discourse,
  But mount you presently, and meet with me              45
  Upon the rising of the mountain foot
  That leads toward Mantua, whither they are fled.
  Dispatch, sweet gentlemen, and follow me.                   [*exit.*
THU. Why, this it is to be a peevish girl

That flies her fortune when it follows her.　　　　50
I'll after, more to be reveng'd on Eglamour
Than for the love of reckless Silvia.　　　　　　*[exit.*
PRO. And I will follow, more for Silvia's love
　　　Than hate of Eglamour, that goes with her.　　　*[exit.*
JUL. And I will follow, more to cross that love　　　55
　　　Than hate for Silvia, that is gone for love.　　*[exit.*

The cupids emerge
from hiding and
continue their
sweeping.

SCENE III.　*The frontiers of Mantua.　The forest.*

*Enter* OUTLAWS *with* SILVIA.

1 OUT. Come, come.
　　　Be patient ; we must bring you to our captain.
SIL. A thousand more mischances than this one
　　　Have learn'd me how to brook this patiently.
2 OUT. Come, bring her away.　　　　　　　　　5
1 OUT. Where is the gentleman that was with her ?
2 OUT. Being nimble-footed, he hath outrun us,
　　　But Moyses and Valerius follow him.
　　　Go thou with her to the west end of the wood ;
　　　There is our captain ; we'll follow him that's fled.　10
　　　The thicket is beset ; he cannot 'scape.
1 OUT. Come, I must bring you to our captain's cave ;
　　　Fear not ; he bears an honourable mind,
　　　And will not use a woman lawlessly.　　　　14
SIL. O Valentine, this I endure for thee !　　　*[exeunt*

SCENE 22
*Exterior. The Forest.*
*Evening.*
See note 24 (page 89).

SCENE IV.　*Another part of the forest.*

*Enter* VALENTINE.

VAL. How use doth breed a habit in a man !
　　　This shadowy desert, unfrequented woods,
　　　I better brook than flourishing peopled towns.
　　　Here can I sit alone, unseen of any,
　　　And to the nightingale's complaining notes　　5
　　　Tune my distresses and record my woes.
　　　O thou that dost inhabit in my breast,
　　　Leave not the mansion so long tenantless,
　　　Lest, growing ruinous, the building fall
　　　And leave no memory of what it was !　　　　10
　　　Repair me with thy presence, Silvia :
　　　Thou gentle nymph, cherish thy forlorn swain.
　　　What halloing and what stir is this to-day ?
　　　These are my mates, that make their wills their law,
　　　Have some unhappy passenger in chase.　　　15
　　　They love me well ; yet I have much to do
　　　To keep them from uncivil outrages.
　　　Withdraw thee, Valentine. Who's this comes here ?　*[steps aside.*

SCENE 23
*Exterior. Another Part
of the Forest, by
Valentine's Cave.
Night. Moonrise.*

*Enter* PROTEUS, SILVIA, *and* JULIA *as* SEBASTIAN.

PRO. Madam, this service I have done for you,
　　　Though you respect not aught your servant doth,　20
　　　To hazard life, and rescue you from him
　　　That would have forc'd your honour and your love.

Vouchsafe me, for my meed, but one fair look;
A smaller boon than this I cannot beg,
And less than this, I am sure, you cannot give.                    25
VAL. [*aside.*]  How like a dream is this I see and hear!
Love, lend me patience to forbear awhile.
SIL.  O miserable, unhappy that I am!
PRO.  Unhappy were you, madam, ere I came;
But by my coming I have made you happy.                           30
SIL.  By thy approach thou mak'st me most unhappy.
JUL. [*aside.*]  And me, when he approacheth to your presence.
SIL.  Had I been seized by a hungry lion,
I would have been a breakfast to the beast
Rather than have false Proteus rescue me.                         35
O, heaven be judge how I love Valentine,
Whose life's as tender to me as my soul!
And full as much, for more there cannot be,
I do detest false, perjur'd Proteus.
Therefore be gone; solicit me no more.                           40
PRO.  What dangerous action, stood it next to death,
Would I not undergo for one calm look?
O, 'tis the curse in love, and still approv'd,
When women cannot love where they're belov'd!
SIL.  When Proteus cannot love where he's belov'd!                45
Read over Julia's heart, thy first best love.
For whose dear sake thou didst then rend thy faith
Into a thousand oaths; and all those oaths
Descended into perjury, to love me.
Thou hast no faith left now, unless thou'dst two,                 50
And that's far worse than none; better have none
Than plural faith, which is too much by one.
Thou counterfeit to thy true friend!
PRO.                          In love,
Who respects friend?
SIL.                          All men but Proteus.
PRO.  Nay, if the gentle spirit of moving words                  55
Can no way change you to a milder form,
I'll woo you like a soldier, at arms' end,
And love you 'gainst the nature of love—force ye.
SIL.  O heaven!
PRO.  I'll force thee yield to my desire.
VAL.  Ruffian! let go that rude uncivil touch;                   60
Thou friend of an ill fashion!
PRO.                          Valentine!
VAL.  Thou common friend, that's without faith or love—
For such is a friend now; treacherous man,
Thou hast beguil'd my hopes; nought but mine eye
Could have persuaded me.  Now I dare not say                     65
I have one friend alive: thou wouldst disprove me.
Who should be trusted, when one's own right hand
Is perjured to the bosom?  Proteus,
I am sorry I must never trust thee more,
But count the world a stranger for thy sake.                     70
The private wound is deepest.  O time most accurst!
'Mongst all foes that a friend should be the worst!

PRO. My shame and guilt confounds me.
  Forgive me, Valentine ; if hearty sorrow
  Be a sufficient ransom for offence,                                75
  I tender 't here ; I do as truly suffer
  As e'er I did commit.
VAL.                    Then I am paid ;
  And once again I do receive thee honest.
  Who by repentance is not satisfied
  Is nor of heaven nor earth, for these are pleas'd ;               80
  By penitence th' Eternal's wrath's appeas'd.
  And, that my love may appear plain and free,
  All that was mine in Silvia I give thee.
JUL. O me unhappy !                          [swoons.
PRO. Look to the boy.                                               85
VAL. Why, boy ! why, wag ! how now !
  What's the matter ?  Look up ; speak.
JUL. O good sir, my master charg'd me to deliver a ring to Madam
  Silvia, which, out of my neglect, was never done.                90
PRO. Where is that ring, boy ?
JUL. Here 'tis ; this is it.
PRO. How ! let me see.  Why, this is the ring I gave to Julia.
JUL. O, cry you mercy, sir, I have mistook ;
  This is the ring you sent to Silvia.                              95
PRO. But how cam'st thou by this ring ?
  At my depart I gave this unto Julia.
JUL. And Julia herself did give it me ;
  And Julia herself have brought it hither.
PRO. How !  Julia !                                                100
JUL. Behold her that gave aim to all thy oaths,
  And entertain'd 'em deeply in her heart.
  How oft hast thou with perjury cleft the root !
  O Proteus, let this habit make thee blush !
  Be thou asham'd that I have took upon me                         105
  Such an immodest raiment—if shame live
  In a disguise of love.
  It is the lesser blot, modesty finds,
  Women to change their shapes than men their minds.
PRO. Than men their minds ! 'tis true.  O heaven, were man  110
  But constant, he were perfect !  That one error
  Fills him with faults ; makes him run through all th' sins :
  Inconstancy falls off ere it begins.
  What is in Silvia's face but I may spy
  More fresh in Julia's with a constant eye ?                      115
VAL. Come, come, a hand from either.
  Let me be blest to make this happy close ;
  'Twere pity two such friends should be long foes.
PRO. Bear witness, heaven, I have my wish for ever.
JUL. And I mine.                                                   120

                    *Enter* OUTLAWS, *with* DUKE *and* THURIO.

OUT. A prize, a prize, a prize !
VAL. Forbear, forbear, I say ; it is my lord the Duke.
  Your Grace is welcome to a man disgrac'd,
  Banished Valentine.

DUKE.                          Sir Valentine !
THU. Yonder is Silvia ; and Silvia's mine.                              125
VAL. Thurio, give back, or else embrace thy death ;
    Come not within the measure of my wrath ;
    Do not name Silvia thine ; if once again,
    Verona shall not hold thee.   Here she stands
    Take but possession of her with a touch—                            130
    I dare thee but to breathe upon my love.
THU. Sir Valentine, I care not for her, I ;
    I hold him but a fool that will endanger
    His body for a girl that loves him not.
    I claim her not, and therefore she is thine.                        135
DUKE. The more degenerate and base art thou
    To make such means for her as thou hast done
    And leave her on such slight conditions.
    Now, by the honour of my ancestry,
    I do applaud thy spirit, Valentine,                                 140
    And think thee worthy of an empress' love.
    Know then, I here forget all former griefs,
    Cancel all grudge, repeal thee home again,
    Plead a new state in thy unrivall'd merit,
    To which I thus subscribe : Sir Valentine,                         145
    Thou art a gentleman, and well deriv'd ;
    Take thou thy Silvia, for thou hast deserv'd her.
VAL. I thank your Grace ; the gift hath made me happy.
    I now beseech you, for your daughter's sake,
    To grant one boon that I shall ask of you.                          150
DUKE. I grant it for thine own, whate'er it be.
VAL. These banish'd men, that I have kept withal,                    See note 25 (page 89).
    Are men endu'd with worthy qualities ;
    Forgive them what they have committed here,
    And let them be recall'd from their exile :                         155
    They are reformed, civil, full of good,
    And fit for great employment, worthy lord.
DUKE. Thou hast prevail'd ; I pardon them, and thee ;
    Dispose of them as thou know'st their deserts.
    Come, let us go ; we will include all jars                          160
    With triumphs, mirth, and rare solemnity.
VAL. And, as we walk along, I dare be bold
    With our discourse to make your Grace to smile.
    What think you of this page, my lord ?
DUKE. I think the boy hath grace in him ; he blushes.                   165
VAL. I warrant you, my lord—more grace than boy.
DUKE. What mean you by that saying ?
VAL. Please you, I'll tell you as we pass along,
    That you will wonder what hath fortuned.
    Come, Proteus, 'tis your penance but to hear                        170
    The story of your loves discovered.
    That done, our day of marriage shall be yours ;
    One feast, one house, one mutual happiness !          [exeunt.

See note 26 (page 89).

# PRODUCTION NOTES

## Don Taylor

1. SCENE 1
   A group of singers and musicians perform a madrigal by
   Orazio Vecchi in Italian from a tower. Beneath them Eglamour and Mercatio bow before Julia and her father, as suitors
   for her hand. Eglamour unrolls a long scroll showing his
   family tree. Mercatio opens an ornamental box and money
   showers out.

2. SCENE 2
   In his study Proteus sits looking down on the preceding
   action, while Valentine sits with his feet up toying with a
   book. Proteus turns to speak but Valentine speaks first.

3. In order to make sense of this passage and to try to make it
   funny, the actors spoke as follows:

   *Proteus.* But what said she?
   *Speed.* Mmm. [*nodding*]
   *Proteus.* Mmm? [*nodding*]
   *Speed.* Ay.
   *Proteus.* Mmm, ay? Why, that's 'noddy'.

4. SCENE 3
   Speed crosses the courtyard as the servants of Julia's father
   shovel Mercatio's money back into the ornamental box.
   Lucetta and Julia in the background climb the steps to Julia's
   tower room.

5. SCENE 5
   In his study Lucetta gives Proteus a letter from Julia. Proteus
   kisses it and tips Lucetta who leaves, putting the money in her
   bodice. Crossing the courtyard below, she smiles at a lutenist
   who is sitting improvising on the steps. She exits and Antonio
   enters, shooing the lutenist away as he offers to play for him.
   Antonio sees his brother speaking to Panthino under an arch.
   His brother goes.

6. SCENE 6
   In his study Proteus soliloquises over Julia's letter. Antonio
   and Panthino are in the courtyard below, looking up at him.
   Proteus goes down to join them.

7. The lutenist plays and sings a setting adapted from music by
   W. Corkine of the first quatrain of Marlowe's 'Come live with
   me and be my love'. Proteus smiles, tips him and runs back up
   to his study.

8. SCENE 7
   The Garden of Love. A golden cupid fires an arrow into a
   shield inscribed 'Amor', held by a statue of Venus. A lutenist
   sings 'When to her lute Corrina sings' by Thomas Campion,
   dancers move gracefully to lute divisions, and a poet nails his
   amorous verses to an ornamental tree. Silvia, seen only by the
   hem of her dress and one ornamental sandal, drops her glove.
   Speed runs and picks it up, then takes it to Valentine who is
   listening to the lutenist.

9. 'Oh that she could speak now like a wood woman.'
   The Folio gives 'would-woman' which makes no sense.
   'Wood' in Elizabethan English is commonplace for 'mad'. The
   line might therefore mean, 'Oh if only this shoe could speak,
   as a mad woman speaks', i.e. strangely, wisely.
       Ellen Dryden suggested to me, after the production, that if
   Launce's shoe had a wooden sole – wooden shoes being a sign
   of poverty, low status – any half-decent comedian could have
   got a laugh simply by knocking on the shoe as he said 'wood
   woman', thus creating a pun. Shakespeare uses the same pun
   in Demetrius' mouth in *Midsummer Night's Dream* II i 192:
   'wood within this wood'. This is a reading I would like to try
   in some future production.
       For the sake of dramatic simplicity we added the verb
   'weeping' and changed 'wood' to 'wild', so that Launce said:
   'Oh that she could speak now, weeping like a wild woman'.
   This way the sentence becomes part of Launce's description of
   the wild and tearful scene at his parting. This is probably not
   what Shakespeare meant, but it made the section playable,
   which as it stands it hardly is.

10. SCENE 9
    Silvia enters to music, showered with rose petals by the
    cupids. Thurio and Valentine with their attendants meet her

there, bow, and all three sit formally.

Speed exits much later, at line 82. When the Duke leaves, Valentine dismisses him with a wave of his hand.

11. The light darkens, thunder is heard, and cupids, poets and musicians flee as a cold wind blows through the Garden of Love, tearing the blossoms from the trees. Having crammed this scene with visualisations of literary images, I used the most ubiquitous literary conceit, the pathetic fallacy – the idea that nature mirrors one's own feelings – at this climactic moment, to mark the onset of Proteus' villainy.

12. Launce, with his dog, takes shelter under an arch from the threatening weather. Speed joins him.

'Welcome to Padua.' One of the play's more hilarious confusions of place. Launce has just arrived in Milan with Proteus. Nobody, as far as we know, has contemplated going to Padua. It might have been some kind of comedian's gag, or more likely it is some kind of mistake or oversight, either on Shakespeare's part or the printers'. We tried to make it work as a gag, but could not discover any satisfactory business to justify the confusion. So I changed the line to 'Welcome to the court'.

13. SCENE 12

A musician sits under a lantern on the steps, playing sad music on an orpharion. Lucetta comes to listen and throws him a red rose. He smiles at her. Up on the gallery of her tower Julia also listens to the music, then seems to reach a decision and hurries down to consult Lucetta.

14. 'There is a lady, in Verona here.'

Another impenetrable confusion of place, uttered by the Duke of Milan in his own court. There was no way of making sense of this and it was changed to 'in the city here'.

15. 'But say this weed her love from Valentine . . .'

Peter Alexander follows the Folio text here. I prefer Knightley's conjectural emendation 'wind' and used it. Shakespeare usually keeps his images coherent, and the image of a weaver winding his skein of wool and 'bottoming it', i.e. tying it off, 'lest it should ravel' follows in the next speech. It would make good dramatic sense that the foolish Thurio should pick up one of Proteus' images and run it into the ground with overuse – yet another comment on the technique of poets and bad poetry which is such a main part of this scene. Conversely, it seems highly *unlikely* that Shakespeare would mix his metaphors so completely from one speech to the next, as the Folio suggests.

16. SCENE 15
The forest setting was stylised, an arrangement of rostra, tall silver poles and ornamental hangings with slanted beams of light falling between them. A shadowy and strange place.

17. The musicians were a full Elizabethan mixed consort: violin, flute, bass viol, lute, cittern and bandora. The song was sung by Proteus himself, and all the music in this scene was performed 'live' during the action, not prerecorded and dubbed.

18. Julia and the Host enter and observe, first from the shelter of an arch, then from the steps leading up to Silvia's Tower.

19. The music for 'Who is Silvia?' was Robert Johnson's setting of 'Have you seen but a bright lily grow' by Ben Jonson, edited and amended by Anthony Rooley to suit Shakespeare's words. The consort then continued to play, first the 'Lachrymae' pavan by John Dowland, then 'Packington's Pound' by that most prolific of composers, Anon.

20. Julia goes through the arch to the foot of Silvia's Tower and meets Silvia hurrying to it. Silvia is unattended. Ursula appears from the Tower with the picture when called (line 113).

21. 'Her eyes are grey as glass, and so are mine.'
The actress playing Julia had brown eyes, and was in close-up at this point. Grey contact lenses were made but looked silly, so the line was finally cut. Such practical limitations would not have troubled Shakespeare. On his stage eye colour was too small a detail to have been seen by the audience, so any of his boy actors could have played the part without trouble. Probably both the boys involved *did* have grey eyes, else why specify that particular point rather than others he might have made?

22. SCENE 21
But the Garden of Love is closed, as it were. The cupids, in their normal street clothes, are sweeping up, and one of the

lutenists is restringing his instrument. Enter Thurio, Proteus and Julia. The cupids and musicians hurriedly scatter.

23.             '. . . she did intend confession
At Patrick's cell this even; and there she was not.'
She was. This line directly contradicts the action of the previous scene, where Eglamour specifically says he is at Patrick's cell. To cover this inconsistency, at the end of the previous scene Eglamour gave Patrick a large purse and whispered 'Shh'. Patrick took the money, grinned and replied 'Shh', suggesting that he will tell the Duke something less than the truth, having received a heavy bribe for the favour.

24. SCENE 22
To the music of John Dowland's 'Battle Galliard' Sir Eglamour comes into the forest, guarding the masked Silvia. The outlaws swing down on ropes from the trees and surround him. He runs away, dropping all his armour in panic as he does so.

25. As they all march away out of the forest, the musicians play 'The Earl of Essex Galliard, Can She Excuse' by John Dowland. The outlaws, the Duke and the lovers join in, all singing heartily.

26. The final captions are accompanied by the music of the Italian madrigal by Orazio Vecchi which opened the production.

# GLOSSARY

## Geoffrey Miles

Difficult phrases are listed under the most important or most difficult word in them. If no such word stands out, they are listed under the first word.

Words appear in the form they take in the text. If they occur in several forms, they are listed under the root form (singular for nouns, infinitive for verbs).

Line references are given only when the same word is used in different places with different meanings. In the case of puns, the senses are distinguished as (i), (ii), etc. Where a word is used punningly several times in succession with a different meaning each time, the senses are given in order of appearance.

Line numbers of prose passages are counted from the last numbered line before the line referred to (since the numbers do not always correspond with the lineation of this edition).

A.B.C., a schoolboy's first reading primer
ABODE, 'makes abode', is living
ABOUT IT, get on with it; 'even now about it', get on with it right now
ABOVE, on a raised place on the Elizabethan stage (perhaps a gallery at the rear of the stage), IV ii 80 *stage direction*; 'above the rest', more than any other reason
ABRIDGE, shorten
ABROAD, away from home (not necessarily 'overseas')
ACCORDS, agrees
ACCOUNT OF, *see* COUNT, II i 55
ADMIRED, wondered at
ADORE, worship
ADVANTAGE (v.), do good to, III ii 42
ADVENTURE, risk
ADVICE, thought, consideration, II iv 203–4, III i 73
AFFECT, am in love with; 'stand affected to', am in love with (*see also* SET); 'how stand you affected to', how do you feel about
AFFECTION, love, passion (stronger than the modern sense)
AFTER-LOVE, love which develops later
AGAIN, (often) back; in return, II i 154
AGE, 'clothe mine age with', acquire as a benefit for my mature years

AGONE, ago (an old-fashioned word)
AGOOD, in earnest
AIM, guess, III i 28; 'aimed at', guessed at; 'gave aim to', was the object of
ALE, alehouse, tavern, II v 49
ALL THESE, (i.e. 'oaths' and 'tears'), II vii 72
ALLYCHOLLY, (an uneducated version of 'melancholy')
ALONE, (i) unique, (ii) 'let her alone', stop talking about her, II iv 163
ALONG, come along, III i 256
AN IF, if
ANGERLY, angrily
ANOTHER THING, (i.e. her sexual favours), III i 341–2
ANTHEM, 'ending anthem', requiem, final song of mourning
APPARENT, clear, obvious
APPLAUD, approve of, I iii 48
APPROACH, (i) arrival, (ii) advances, V iv 31
APPROVED, 'still approved', continually being proved true
ARIADNE, in Greek mythology, a Cretan princess who fell in love with the Athenian hero Theseus when he came as a prisoner to Crete, and helped him penetrate the Labyrinth and kill the Minotaur. Theseus took her with him in his escape from Crete, but abandoned her

on the island of Naxos and sailed on to Athens without her

ARM, 'at arm's end', with the point of my weapon (i.e. sword, but perhaps with a sexual pun)

ARTICLE, item on the list

AS, like, I ii 114, III ii 6; that, II iv 133, IV iv 103

ASTRAY, wrong (punning on 'a stray (sheep)')

AT LARGE, fully

ATTEND (ON), wait for, III i 186, IV iii 5; 'attended', watched, V i 10

AUGHT, anything

AUGURY, skill in interpreting signs

AWFUL, law-abiding, having respect ('awe') for authority

BAA, (punning on 'bah!')

BADE, told to

BARE, (i) threadbare, (ii) mere, II iv 42; (i) mere, (ii) naked (as opposed to the hairy spaniel), III i 269

BASE, see BASS, I ii 97

BASS, BASE, (a series of puns) (i) bass voice, (ii) base or despicable person, (iii) 'bid the base' (a term from the children's game Prisoner's Base, in which one player challenges the rest to chase him or her, to give the 'prisoner' in the 'base' a chance to escape; Lucetta is attracting Julia's anger to give Proteus a chance), I ii 96–7

BEADSMAN, one paid to pray on behalf of others

BEAR, 'bear with', (i) put up with, (ii) act as bearer for, I i 115–6; 'bear a hard opinion', hold a low opinion; 'bears an honourable mind', has an honourable character

BEAUTY, 'beauty . . . kindness', i.e. beauty only flourishes when accompanied by kindness

BECAME THEM, suited them

BECHANCE, befall, come

BECOME, suit, be appropriate for, II vii 47, III ii 86; 'shall become you well', makes you well suited, IV ii 125

BEFORTUNE, befall, come to

BEGUIL'D, cheated, disappointed

BEHOLDING, indebted

BELIKE (THAT), probably, presumably

BESEEM, be suitable for

BESET, surrounded, V iii 11; 'hard beset', under heavy attack (by suitors)

BESHREW ME, (a mild oath)

BESTOW MYSELF, behave

BETIDETH, happens (to)

BETTER, i.e. more willing, III ii 19

BIDING, 'of biding there', that she would remain there (if she was uncooperative)

BIDS, tells to

BLACK, dark-complexioned, swarthy (regarded as ugly according to the Elizabethan standard of blonde, fair-skinned beauty), III i 103, IV iv 152, V ii 10–12; 'Though ne'er so black', though they may be as dark as ever a woman was

BLACK'ST, worst (with a pun on the literal sense)

BLASTING, being blighted

BLESS THE MARK, (a formula used to excuse saying something offensive)

BLIND, 'Love is blind', see LOVE

BLOOD, 'of blood', (i) of noble birth, (ii) of spirit

BLOT, disgrace

BLOW, blooms

BLUNT, dull-witted

BOON, favour

BOOTS, (a series of puns) (i) 'over boots', in deep (the water up to your knees), (ii) 'give me not the boots', don't make fun of me (slang), (iii) 'boots thee not', does you no good, I i 25–8

BOSOM, i.e. heart, V iv 68; (Elizabethan women often carried letters and love-tokens in a pocket inside the bodice), III i 144

BOTTOM, rewind, as onto a bottom (a spool around which thread was wound). Silvia's love is envisaged as a thread being wound from one spool (Valentine) to another (Thurio)

BRAGGARDISM, arrogant boastfulness

BREAK, 'break with', reveal our intentions to; 'break with thee of', reveal to you; 'break my fast', breakfast; 'break . . . hours', fail to keep appointments

BREAST, i.e. heart

BREATH, 'here's my mother's breath' (Launce is presumably making the shoe squeak by pressing it 'up and down')

BREED, bring about

BRING, (often) go along with

BROKEN, 'are they broken', have they split up? (but Launce takes the word literally)

BROOK, endure, tolerate

BURDEN, (i) load, (ii) refrain in the bass, sung throughout a song, I ii 85

BUT, (often) only; (often) except; 'but is', that is not; 'but that she will', that she will not;

'but I can', that I cannot; 'but now', only just now

BY, about, II iv 147; beside (me), III i 175, 178

CALL, (i) summon, (ii) call names (Launce's misunderstanding), II iii 50–1
CALM, i.e. gentle, V iv 42
CAME HARDLY OFF, see HARDLY
CAN, can say, II iv 161
CANKER, canker-worm
CAPON'S, chicken's
CAR, chariot
CATE-LOG, catalogue (with a pun on 'Kate' as a common name for a prostitute?)
CAVIL AT, criticise
CENSURE, pass judgement
CHAF'D, angered
CHAMBER, room
CHAMELEON, (which according to legend lived on a diet of air alone)
CHANGE, (i) variation, modulation (in the music), (ii) alteration (in Proteus's feelings), IV ii 66–7
CHANGING, fickle
CHARACTER'D, inscribed
CHARG'D, ordered, V iv 89
CHASE, 'have . . . in chase', are in pursuit of
CHECK, restrain
CHID (AT), scolded, rebuked
CHIDDEN, scolded
CHIDE, rebuke; scold, III i 98
CHOOSE, help
CHRONICLED FOR, set down as, called
CIRCUMSTANCE, (i) chain of reasoning, (ii) situation, I i 36–7; chain of reasoning, I i 82; circumstantial details, III ii 36
CITE, urge, II iv 81
CIVIL, civilised
CLERKLY, in a scholarly manner
CLOISTER, colonnaded avenue (not necessarily in a monastery)
CLOS'D, embraced
CLOSE (adj.), enclosed, confined, III i 235; (n.) (i) union, (ii) conclusion, V iv 117
CLOSEST, most tightly confined; 'Fire . . . all' (proverbial)
CODPIECE, a pouch in the front of a man's breeches, covering the genitals (often, in Elizabethan fashion, stuffed to impressive size and used 'to stick pins on')
COIL, fuss, disturbance
COLD, 'suit will be but cold', wooing will be unsuccessful

COLOUR, pretence
COMMAND ME, call on me for favours, III i 23
COMMEND, offer, I iii 42, IV ii 9; 'commend . . . will', offer their service to do whatever he wishes; 'Commend they grievance to', entrust your trouble to the care of; 'have them much commended', send their warmest regards
COMMENDATIONS, greetings
COMMIT, sin
COMMON, (i) base, (ii) ordinary, like all the rest (Proteus's treachery has disillusioned Valentine with all 'friends')
COMPASS (n.), width, II vii 51; (v.) obtain, II iv 210; 'compass yours', (Proteus plays on different meanings of 'will': (i) accomplish your wishes for you, (ii) win your goodwill, (iii) arouse your sexual desire), IV ii 88
COMPETITOR, (i) associate, (ii) rival (an ironic second meaning)
COMPOSED, carefully constructed
CONCEIT, opinion
CONCEITLESS, unintelligent
CONCERNS, is of importance, I ii 77
CONCORD, harmony
CONDITION, characteristics; 'such slight conditions', such easy terms
CONFOUNDS, puts to shame, throws into confusion
CONJURE, entreat
CONSORT, band of musicians, III ii 84; 'of our consort', one of our band (of outlaws)
CONSTANCY, 'for my true constancy', as a pledge of my faithfulness
CONSTANT, steadfast, unchanging, consistently faithful
CONTEMNING, feeling contempt for
CONTINUE LOVE TO HIM, continue to be in love with him
CONTRARY, perverse, IV iv 79; see INSTANCE, II iv 15
CONVERS'D, associated with each other
CORRECTION, punishment
COUNSEL (n.), advice; (v.) advise; 'Myself in counsel', with myself in the secret
COUNT, consider, V iv 70; 'out of count', (i) infinite, (ii) too trivial to be counted, II i 50–1; 'counts of', values; 'account of', value
COUNTERFEIT TO THY TRUE FRIEND, false pretender to friendship with the man who was truly your friend
COY, disdainful
CRAB, (i.e. crab-apple, suggesting that Crab is 'the sourest-natured dog')

CROOKED, malicious
CROSS, thwart; 'cross'd with', thwarted by
CRUSTS, 'I love crusts' (i.e. and he will not have to share them with her)
CRY YOU MERCY, I beg your pardon
CURRISH, rude and snarling
CURST, (i) shrewish, (ii) savage (of an animal)

DEADLY, like death, III i 173
DEAR, loving, IV iii 14
DEARTH, famine
DEEP, DEEPER, profound(er) (with a pun on the literal sense), I i 21–3
DEIGN, condescend to receive
DELIVER, speak, III ii 35
DELIVER'D, who gave, IV iv 69
DEPART (n.), departure, V iv 97
DEPENDING, relying
DEPLORING, see DUMP
DERIV'D, descended; (i) descended (in ancestry), (ii) come down in the world (pun), V ii 23–4
DESERT, wild uninhabited place, V iv 2; 'not without desert . . . reputed', i.e. he deserves his good reputation; 'good desert', deserving good opinion
DESPERATE, in despair
DESTIN'D TO A DRIER DEATH, (alluding to the proverb that 'He that is born to be hanged shall never be drowned')
DETERMINE, 'determin'd of', is decided upon; 'determine our proceedings', decide what we are going to do
DEVOTED, 'else devoted', vowed to someone else
DIE ON, fight to the death against
DIET, 'takes diet', is on a diet (for medical reasons)
DIGNIFY, bring honour to
DIN'D, (i.e. on the sight of Silvia), II i 159
DIRECTION-GIVER, one who directs the aim of an archer or gunner
DISABILITY, lack of ability or worth (see LEAVE)
DISCIPLINE, lesson, training
DISCOURSE, conversation, talk
DISCOVER, (usually) reveal
DISCOVERY, 'my discovery', the fact that I revealed (the plan)
DISCRETION, judgment, good sense
DISFURNISH, deprive
DISGRAC'D, (punning on 'Grace'), V iv 123
DISPATCH, make haste, V ii 48
DISPOSE, disposal, II vii 86, IV i 76

DISPRAISE (n.), 'his dispraise', condemnation of him; (v.) criticise, condemn
DOG, 'a dog at', adept at (a proverbial phrase, but with a pun on the literal sense)
DOLOUR, grief, pain
DOOM, sentence; 'deadly doom', sentence of death; 'to the doom', in opposition to the sentence
DOUBLET, a short, close-fitting man's jacket
DOUBT, 'makes no doubt of', has no doubts about (a pointedly ambiguous remark)
DOUBTFULLY, uncertainly
DREAM, 'dream on thee', think about you; 'dream on infamy', worry about the damage to your reputation
DRIFT, scheme
DUCAT, a gold or silver Italian coin, worth about 3s 6d
DULL PROCEEDING, stupid plans
DUMP, 'tune a deploring dump', sing a doleful melancholy tune
DUTY, dutifulness, loyalty

EARNEST, 'perceive her earnest', (i) think that she was serious, (ii) see her down-payment to seal a bargain (i.e. the letter)
EFFECT (v.), bring about
EFFECTS, 'fair effects of future hopes', fine fulfilment of hopes for the future
EFFECTUAL, 'which . . . effectual force', which, since it has not been reversed, remains in effect
EGLAMOUR, (the character referred to at I i 9 is apparently not the same person as Silvia's friend in Milan)
EITHER, each of you (Proteus and Julia), V iv 116
ELEGIES, love poems
ELSE, otherwise, III i 9; 'what news else', whatever other news; 'or fearing else', or else fearing; 'else devoted', see DEVOTED
ELYSIUM, i.e. Heaven (in Greek mythology, the land of blessed souls)
EMPEROR, (Shakespeare sometimes refers to the Duke of Milan as 'Emperor'; presumably he changed his mind about the character's rank while writing or revising the play, and the confusion was never cleared up)
ENAMELL'D, i.e. smooth and shiny
ENCOUNTERS, 'the loose encounters of', being lecherously accosted by
ENDAMAGE, damage, hurt
ENDING, see ANTHEM
ENDU'D, endowed

ENFRANCHISE, set free
ENGINE, device (i.e. the rope-ladder)
ENJOIN'D, requested
ENQUIRE YOU FORTH, find you by asking where you are
ENTERTAIN, take into service, employ (often in the courtly-love sense; *see* SERVANT)
ENTERTAINED, employed, taken into service, IV iv 59, 87; lodged, V iv 102
ENTHRALLED, enslaved
ENVIRON, surround
ERE, before
ESSENCE, very being
ESTEEM (n.), 'good esteem', high reputation; (v.) 'esteemeth as', considers to be; 'nought esteems', cares nothing for; 'How esteem'st thou me?', i.e. Don't I qualify as a 'man'?
ESTIMATION, reputation
ETERNAL, 'th'Eternal', God
ETHIOPE, black African (considered the epitome of ugliness by the Elizabethans)
EVEN, just, exactly (often a meaningless intensifier); 'Even now about it', *see* ABOUT; 'Even as . . . teach a dog', i.e. in precisely the approved technique for teaching dogs; (n.) evening, V ii 42
EVE'S LEGACY, (i.e. the common fault of all women)
EVER, (often) always
EV'N, *see* EVEN
EXCELS, is excellent, IV ii 79
EXCEPT, unless, II iv 136, III i 178; (i) with the exception of, (ii) make an exception of, (iii) take exception to, object to (a series of puns), II iv 150-1; 'excepted most against', raised the greatest impediments to
EXCEPTIONS, 'take exceptions', object; 'takes exceptions at', objects to
EXCHEQUER, treasury
EXCUSE IT NOT, don't make excuses (for not going)
EXERCISE, activity
EXHIBITION, allowance
EXPECTS, awaits
EXPEDITION, haste
EXPOSTULATE, discuss at length
EYE, 'be in eye of', be in a position to observe

FAIN, content, I i 115; 'would fain', would like to
FAIR, (often) beautiful, handsome; (i) handsome, (ii) fair-complexioned, V ii 9-10; kindly, V iv 23
FAITH, honesty, loyalty, fidelity

FALSE, (often) treacherous, unfaithful; 'plays false', *see* PLAY
FANTASTIC, whimsical, fanciful
FARTHINGALE, hooped petticoat
FASHION, 'ill fashion', bad kind; 'fashion me', adapt myself
FASTING, i.e. before she has eaten
FAULT, 'take a fault upon me', take the blame for something
FAULTS, crimes, IV i 53
FAVOUR, graciousness, charm, II i 49
FEAR ME, fear
FEATURE, appearance
FEE, 'more fee', a better reward
FEELING, full of emotion
FIE, (an exclamation of impatience or disapproval)
FIGURE, (i) rhetorical device, (ii) number (as opposed to 'letter'), II i 137-9
FIND, find out, III i 31
FIRE, spark (to fire the guns for the 'volley'), II iv 34
FIT, supply, II vii 42; 'fits as well as', is as incongruous as; 'served me as fit', fitted me as well
FITTING WELL, very appropriate for
FLAT, (i) the musical sense, (ii) downright, blunt, I ii 93
FLATTER, (i) pay false compliments to, (ii) encourage in pleasant illusions, II iv 143-4; (i) 'flatter'd', was too kind to, (ii) 'flatter with myself', delude myself, IV iv 183-4
FLOOD, tide
FLY, 'I fly not . . . doom', I am not escaping death if I escape from the Duke's sentence of death (because absence from Silvia is in itself death)
FOLD, multiply (with a pun on 'pinfold'), I i 104
FOND, foolish
FOOL, 'poor fool' (referring to herself), IV iv 89
FOOLS, (i.e. women in general), III i 99
FOR, (often) as; (often) because; as a pledge of, II ii 8; because of, IV i 50; by, when she says, III i 101; 'for catching cold', in case they catch cold; 'for my love', (i) in return for my love, (ii) to be my love (instead of you); 'for thine own', as yours
FOR WHY, because
FORBEAR, wait, restrain oneself, II vii 14, V iv 27; don't do it, III i 102; stop, V iv 122
FORCE, rape, V iv 58; 'forc'd your honour', i.e. raped you
FOREHEAD, (a high forehead was regarded by

the Elizabethans as beautiful)
FORGOT, forgotten how, III i 85
FORSWEAR, perjure
FORSWORN, perjured, an oathbreaker, II vi
1–3, IV ii 10; renounced, abandoned, III i
212–4, III ii 4
FORTUNE, good fortune (of sleeping in Silvia's bosom), III i 147; (i.e. the chance of
marrying Thurio), V ii 50; luck, IV i 43
FORTUNED, happened
FORWARD, advanced in growth, I i 45; bold,
cheeky (but Speed pretends to take it as
'prompt'), II i 11
FRAME, compose
FREE, generous, magnanimous
FRESH, blooming
FRIENDS, (sometimes) relatives
FULL, fully, III i 76; just, IV iv 182, V iv 38
FULL-FRAUGHT, fully laden
FURNISH, equip

GAVE, 'gave me . . . oath', made me take the
oath
GENTLE, (often) noble
GET THEE HENCE, go away
GIVE, 'give her o'er', give up on her; 'give
back', back off
GIVER, (i) direction-giver (see DIRECTION),
(ii) provider of Thurio's inspiration
GO, walk, IV ii 20; (i) make my way, (ii) walk;
III i 366–8
GO TO, (an impatient exclamation: 'enough of
this!')
GOODLY, excellent (ironical), I ii 41; 'goodly
shape', handsome appearance
GOSSIPS, either (i) women visitors during her
confinement, or (ii) godparents at her child's
baptism (in either case, the implication is that
she has had an illegitimate child)
GOVERN, see STARS
GRACE (n.), (i) graciousness, (ii) favour, III i
146; good or pleasing qualities, IV ii 41; (i)
sense of propriety, (ii) (feminine) gracefulness, V iv 165–6; 'your Grace' (the Duke's
title); 'grace to grace', pleasing qualities
which do credit to; (v.) honour, dignify, II ii
18, II iv 70
GRACED, honoured
GRACES, charms, good qualities
GRACIOUS, acceptable, III i 357
GRANDAM, grandmother
'GREED, agreed
GREY AS GLASS, (a conventional formula;
'grey' probably means blue)

GRIEFS, grievances
GRIEVANCE(S), suffering, distress
GRIEVOUSLY, with great grief

HABILIMENTS, clothes
HABIT, costume, II vii 39, V iv 104
HAD, would have, II iv 78, II iv 84, IV iv 12–13
HAIR, 'there's not a hair . . . Valentine', he is
Valentine (or a true lover) in every particular
(with a pun on 'hare'?)
HALIDOM, 'by my halidom' (a mild, old-
fashioned oath)
HALLOING, shouting
HALLOWMAS, All Saints' Day (1 November), a day on which charity was traditionally
handed out to the poor
HAMMERING, pondering, brooding
HAP, fortune, luck
HAPLESS, unfortunate
HAPLY, perhaps, II iv 12, III i 25; as it
happens, I i 12, 32; 'If haply won', see IF
HAPPY, bearing good news, II iv 49; skilful,
IV i 34; 'happy being', happiness
HARBOUR, give shelter to, I ii 42; lodge, stay,
III i 140, 149
HARD, 'It shall go hard but', I guarantee that;
'goes hard', is painful, is hard to take, IV iv 2
HARD-FAVOURED, ugly
HARDLY, with difficulty, I i 126; 'came hardly
off', was done with difficulty
HARK, listen
HAVE, get, III i 122; who have, V iv 15
HAZARD, risk
HEARD, 'He heard not that' (i.e. he will
pretend not to have heard it)
HEARKEN, listen
HEARTY, heartfelt
HEAVIEST, 'most heaviest', saddest
HEAVY, serious (punning on the literal sense),
I ii 84; depressed, III ii 62
HEEDFULLY, upon mature consideration
HELD ME GLAD, considered myself glad (to
get off so easily)
HELLESPONT, the Bosphorus (see LEANDER)
HENCE, away (from here)
HERO, the lover of LEANDER
HIE, hurry
HIE YOU, hurry
HIMSELF, he himself, III i 143
HOLD, consider, II vi 29, V iv 133; take that
(Silvia tears the letter up and gives it back to
Julia), IV iv 123; 'hold thee', i.e. keep you
safe from me, V iv 129; 'hold excus'd', excuse

HOLE, 'shoe with the hole in it' (a bawdy joke)

HOLY, virtuous

HOME-KEEPING, stay-at-home

HOMELY, simple, I i 2

HORNS, (alluding to the old joke that horns grew on the forehead of a cuckolded husband – though Valentine's horns can only be potential ones), I i 78

HOSE, men's stockings or breeches; 'round hose', a type of breeches puffed out around the hips

HOST, landlord of an inn (at which Julia is staying)

HOSTESS, landlady of a tavern

HOUR, 'this hour', an hour from now

HOW, 'how say'st thou that', what do you say about the fact that

HOW NOW, (an expression of greeting, or of surprise or disapproval: 'what's going on?')

HOWEVER, in any case, whatever happens, I i 34

IF, 'If haply won . . . labour won', If you happen to win the girl, you may wish you hadn't, and if you lose her, you have gained nothing but pain and trouble; 'if thou hast sinned', i.e. if I have sinned in following your (Love's) instructions; 'if I should speak it', even if I should say so myself; 'if once again', if you do so (call her yours) once more

ILL, bad, unpleasant, III ii 40, V iv 61; badly, V ii 16

ILL-FAVOURED, unbecoming

IMPEACHMENT TO, reproach to him in

IMPERIAL, (Launce's error for 'Emperor'; see EMPEROR)

IMPORT, 'of much import', very important

IMPORTUNACY, importunity

IMPORTUNE, plead with; 'thither them importune', command them to go there

IMPOSE, command

IMPRESS, impression (on the mind)

IN, into, III i 250; to perform, IV iii 10; 'in the way', at hand

INCLUDE, conclude

INCONSTANCY . . . BEGINS, i.e. the man who lacks constancy loses interest in something even before he has properly begun it

INDIFFERENT, neither good nor bad, morally neutral

INDUSTRY, hard work

INFAMY, see DREAM

INFINITE, infinity

INFLUENCE, (a term from astrology, describing the power of the stars to control human character and destiny)

INHABIT, dwell

INHERIT, gain possession of

INLY, inward

INPRIMIS, (Latin) first of all (the conventional beginning to a list)

INSTANCE, 'What instance of the contrary?', What evidence is there that I am not wise?

INSTANCES, proofs

INTEGRITY, 'such integrity', such single-hearted devotion (as your tears demonstrate)

INTEND, intend to make, IV ii 45, V ii 41

INTEREST, 'he should . . . interest', i.e. the man should outdo the lady in compliments, not vice versa

INTERPRET, see MOTION

ITEM, (the conventional way of introducing an item on a list)

JADE, (i) nag, poor horse, (ii) contemptuous term for a woman

JARS (n.), discords, conflicts, V iv 160; (v.) is discordant, IV ii 65

JEALOUS, suspicious

JERKIN, a long jacket worn over or instead of a doublet

JOLT-HEAD, blockhead

JOY (v.), take pleasure, II iv 123

LAMENTABLE, tragic

LAY, flatten down (by sprinkling with water), II iii 26

LEANDER, a lover who swam every night across the Hellespont (the Bosphorus) to visit his love Hero in her tower, until one night he was drowned in a storm. (Perhaps an allusion to Christopher Marlowe's poem Hero and Leander, written about the same time as the play)

LEARN, teach, II vi 13

LEARN'D, taught, V iii 4

LEASE, 'out by lease', let out to others (presumably Proteus is sarcastically pitying them for not having the privilege of being personally managed by Thurio, but the point of the joke is obscure)

LEAVE, cease, II vi 17–8, III i 182; neglect, I i 65; part with, IV iv 70; 'Leave off . . . disability', stop talking about your own lack of ability; 'Give him leave', make allowances for him; 'give us leave', leave us (a polite form of dismissal)

LEFT, abandoned, IV iv 170

LESSON (v.), instruct

LETS BUT ONE MAY ENTER, prevents one from entering

LETTER, 'this letter' (apparently Julia accidentally gives Silvia one of Proteus's letters to herself – perhaps the letter from I ii, visibly pieced together), IV iv 117

LEVIATHANS, sea monsters

LIBERAL, (i) licentious, indecent, (ii) generous

LIE, (i) lie on the ground, (ii) tell lies, I ii 76–7

LIES, stays, lodges, IV ii 133

LIEU, 'in lieu thereof' (i.e. in exchange for my goods and lands)

LIGHT, i.e. information, III i 49

LIGHT O'LOVE, (a popular song)

LIGHTLY, easily

LIGHTS, power of sight

LIKE, dressed as, II vii 40

LIKELIHOODS, pieces of evidence

LIKES, (i) 'likes you not', does not please you, (ii) 'likes me not', does not love me, IV ii 54–5

LILY-TINCTURE, i.e. white colouring

LIME, birdlime (a sticky substance smeared on branches to entangle small birds)

LIONS, (probably a reference to the captive lions in the Tower of London), II i 24

LIVELY, convincingly

LIVERIES, uniforms (worn by servants of a noble household)

LOATH, reluctant

LOITERER, idler

LONG, (often) for a long time

LOOK, expect, II iv 116; 'have a look of', be given a glance by

LOOK WHAT, whatever, I iii 74

LOOSE, see ENCOUNTERS

LOSE, waste, I i 67

LOVE, (Cupid, the god of love, was traditionally depicted as blind, symbolising – according to one's degree of cynicism – either that lovers are indifferent to externals, or that they are blind to the truth about those they love), II i 63, IV ii 45–6, IV iv 192

LOVE-BOOK, a romance or handbook of courtly love (rather than a prayer-book)

LOVE-DISCOURSE, talk about love

LOVELY, loving (?), I ii 19

LUBBER, coarse lout (punning on 'lover')

LUMPISH, low-spirited

LUSTILY, vigorously

MAID, (a play on the different meanings of the word) (i) girl, (ii) virgin, (iii) maidservant, III i 266–8

MAINTENANCE, allowance

MAKE, 'makes this good', lives up to this description; 'make return', returns; see MEANS, V iv 137

MAN, servant, IV ii 72

MANAGE, wield

MANNERLY, modest (with a pun on 'manly')

MARK, observe, note, II iii 25, IV iv 29

MARRY, (a mild oath: 'by the Virgin Mary')

MASK'D, 'being mask'd', because she was masked

MASTERSHIP, (a jokingly respectful term of address)

MATCH, 'will't be a match', will they get married?

MATES, companions (a contemptuous word), III i 158

MATTER, 'It's no matter for that', that doesn't matter; 'great matter', important business

ME, 'steps me', etc (the 'me' here is meaningless, a habit of colloquial speech), IV iv 7, 13, etc

MEAN, means, way, II vii 5, III i 38; agent, IV iv 104; 'There wanteth but a mean', all you need is (i) a happy medium, (ii) a tenor voice (i.e. Proteus?); 'make such means', take such pains, use such (discreditable) means

MEASURE (n.), reach (literally, the distance within which a fencer could wound his opponent), V iv 127; (v.) 'To measure', in making his way across

MEAT, food

MEED, reward

MEET (adj.), suitable

MERCATIO, (presumably a rich merchant, from Italian mercato, market)

MEROPS' SON, see PHAETHON

METAMORPHIS'D, metamorphosed, transformed

METHINKS, it seems to me (that)

MILK, (i) milk cows, (ii) 'milk' a lover of money or favours (?), III i 293–4

MIND, opinion, I ii 7; intentions, II iv 26, IV iii 2; thoughts, what is in one's mind, I ii 33, II i 155; message, I i 130; 'in telling your mind', when you speak to her in person, I i 131

MINION, hussy

MINISTER, administer

MISTAK'ST ME, misunderstand me (but Launce takes him to mean 'mistake me for someone else')

97

MISTOOK, made a mistake
MOAN, 'the moan she makes' (presumably Launce swishes his staff through the air)
MOIST, moisten
'MONGST, amongst
MONTH'S MIND TO, longing for (such as pregnant women feel)
MOOD, fit of anger
MOTION, puppet-show (in which the actions of the silent puppets were 'interpreted' in a commentary by the puppet-master. Silvia, the 'puppet', unable to speak of her love, is trying to get Valentine to 'interpret' her gesture)
MOUNTAIN-FOOT, foothills
MOV'D, wooed, proposed to, I ii 27
MOVED, 'Be moved', (i) have pity, (ii) get a move on
MOYSES, (a form of 'Moses')
MUSE, wonder, I iii 64; are lost in thought, II i 157
MUST, must go, II iv 172, 183
MUTTON, sheep; 'lac'd mutton', prostitute (a slang phrase, presumably referring to their tightly-laced clothes)
MYSELF, (often) I

NAME, call, V iv 128
NAMELESS, (i) inexpressible, (ii) too trivial to be worth mentioning, (iii) bastard (Launce's interpretation), III i 310
NEAT, elegant
NEEDS, necessarily
NE'ER, never, not at all
NEW-FOUND, newly invented
NICE, unwilling
NICHOLAS, see SAINT NICHOLAS
NICK, 'out of all nick', beyond all reckoning (tavern accounts were kept by 'nicks' or notches on a stick)
NO MORE OF STAY, no more talk of delay
NODDY, fool
NONE ELSE WOULD, i.e. no one else would perceive that you were in love (?)
NOOKS, corners
NOT A WHIT, not at all
NOT SO, (i.e. there is no sign of 'daylight', or hope, for Julia), IV ii 135
NOTE, (i) tune, (ii) short letter, I ii 81
NOUGHT, nothing; see SET, I i 68

OBJECT, sight; 'by a newer object', as a result of a newer sight
ODD-CONCEITED, strangely devised, eccentric

O'ERLOOKED, examined
O'ERNIGHT, overnight
O'ERSLIPS, slips past
OF, for, I ii 110, II iv 129; about, III i 254; by, V iv 4; 'of a puppy', since he was a puppy
OFFICE, 'ill office', unpleasant task
OFT, often
OFTENTIMES, often
OMITTING, neglecting
ON, (often) of
ONE, (punning on 'on', which was pronounced the same way), II i 2; 'that's all one', that doesn't matter; 'if he be but one knave' (the point is obscure, but 'two knaves' seems to have been an Elizabethan phrase describing more-than-normal villainy)
ONSET, 'give the onset', make a start on carrying out
OPEN THE MATTER, reveal the facts
OPPOSES HER AGAINST, opposes
ORACLES, (i.e. as true as messages from the gods)
ORDERLY, properly, in due order
ORPHEUS, the great musician and singer of Greek mythology, whose music could make wild beasts tame; 'Orpheus' lute . . . sinews', i.e. the power of Orpheus' music is that of the poet's words
OVERCHARGED, overcrowded
OVERWEENING, arrogantly presumptuous
OWE, own

PADUA, (apparently Shakespeare's slip for 'Milan'), II v 1
PAGEANTS OF DELIGHT, delightful performances
PAINTED, (i.e. with make-up)
PARABLE, enigmatic saying
PARDON, 'I will pardon you', i.e. I give you permission to go now
PARLE, talk, conversation
PARTAKER, sharer
PARTNER OF HIS FORTUNE, to share his good fortune
PARTS, is leaving
PASSENGER, traveller
PASSING, extreme, excessive, I ii 17, II i 67; extremely, IV iv 144
PASSION, passionate outburst
PASSIONING, passionately grieving
PAWN, pledge; 'pawn for fealty', pledge of loyalty (from another lover)
PEACE, (often) Be quiet; 'hold your peace', remain silent

PEARLS, (i) precious objects ('Black men . . . eyes' is proverbial), (ii) cataracts

PEEVISH, perverse, obstinate

PENTECOST, Whitsuntide (a festival in May, seven weeks after Easter, often the occasion of games and theatrical performances)

PERCEIVE, (i) gather (from her actions), (ii) receive, I i 127–8; see EARNEST, II i 144–5

PERCHANCE, perhaps

PEREMPTORY, resolved

PERIOD, pause at the end of a sentence (i.e. a fine place to pause, after 'and yet')

PERIWIG, 'such a colour'd periwig', a wig of that colour

PERJUR'D TO THE BOSOM, disloyal to the heart

PERPLEXITY, distress

PERSEVERS SO, perseveres, persists in doing so

PERSON, appearance

PERUSE, read over

PHAETHON, in Greek mythology, the son of Phoebus the sun god and a mortal woman, Clymene, wife of Merops. He persuaded Phoebus to let him drive the chariot of the sun across the heavens for a day, but was unable to control the horses; the chariot went out of control, scorching the earth, until Jupiter killed Phaethon with a thunderbolt. He is a type of rash ambition. ('Merops' son' implies that, in the Duke's opinion, Valentine is a mere upstart without even Phaethon's half-share of divine blood)

PICTURE, (perhaps) outward appearance (but some critics think these lines come from an earlier version of the play in which Proteus first fell in love with Silvia from a sight of her portrait), II iv 205

PILLORY, a device, like the stocks, in which the prisoner stood fastened by the arms

PIN, (proverbially worthless)

PINFOLD, pound, an enclosure for stray animals

PISSING WHILE, the time it takes to urinate (a slang phrase for 'a very short time', but literally appropriate in this case)

PLAC'D, 'since I know . . . plac'd', i.e. since I know that the love which causes your distress is virtuously placed (on Valentine)

PLAY, 'plays false', (i) plays out of tune, (ii) is unfaithful; 'one play but one thing', one person play only one part (i.e. remain constant and faithful); 'play the cur', act like a cur (i.e. despicably)

PLEAD A NEW STATE . . . MERIT, argue (as an excuse for changing my mind) that your incomparable merit, now revealed, has created a new state of affairs

PLEASE YOU, please, if it pleases you to

POESY, poetry

POSSESS'D, taken hold of

POST (n.), messenger (punning on 'wooden post'), I i 143; (v.) hurry, II iii 31

POSTERN, small side door

POUND, (a series of puns) (i) enclose in a pound (pen for stray animals), (ii) beat, (iii) the sum of money (Speed's deliberate misunderstanding)

POX OF, a plague upon

PRACTISING, plotting

PRAISE, (i) appraise, test (by sipping), (ii) speak highly of, III i 336–8

PRAY HER TO, ask her to commit

PREFER, (i) show a preference for, (ii) promote, II iv 152–3; press the case of, III ii 4

PREFERMENT, (social) advancement

PREFERR'D, asserted, II vi 15

PRESENTLY, immediately

PRETENCE, intention

PRETENDED, intended

PREVAIL'D, convinced me

PREVENT, avoid

PRICKS ME ON, spurs me, compels me

PRIME, spring

PRINCIPALITY, a type of high-ranking angel (according to some theologians, seventh in the hierarchy of nine orders of angelic beings attending on God)

PRINT, 'in print', (i) plainly, (ii) in a book (these lines may be a quotation, but no source is known)

PRIVATE, (i.e. inflicted by a friend)

PRIVILEGE, 'is privilege for', grants you the privilege of

PRIVY TO, in the knowledge of

PRIZE, 'A prize', a valuable catch

PROCEED, 'thus suddenly proceed', take such sudden action

PRODIGIOUS, (Launce's error for 'Prodigal')

PROPER, handsome, fine-looking

PROPORTION, (Launce's error for 'portion', i.e. inheritance)

PROTEST, declare

PROTEUS, (named after a character in Greek mythology, an Old Man of the Sea who would evade capture by changing himself into many different shapes. The name suggests Proteus' fickleness and changeability)

PROUD, (i) arrogant, (ii) lascivious, III i 327

PROVIDE, prepare

PROVIDED, equipped with what I need, I iii 72

PUBLISHER, one who makes public

PUDDINGS, sausages made of animal intestines stuffed with mincemeat

PULING, in a whining voice

PURPOSED, intended, had it in mind

PUT FORTH, send out (into the world)

RAGGED, rugged

RAIL'D AT, abused

RANSOM, payment to atone for a crime

RAVEL, become entangled

REACH SO HIGH, (i) sing such high notes, (ii) aspire to a man of such high rank

REASON, 'no reason but', no doubt that

REASONING, talking of (but Speed's reply alludes to the traditional phrase 'rhyme or reason')

REASONLESS, irrationally

RECEIVE THEE, consider you, accept you as

RECKING, caring; 'Recking . . . befortune you', i.e. my indifference to my own safety is as great as my concern for your success

RECORD, sing about

RECOURSE, access

RECOVER, reach

REGARD (v.), take account of, III i 255; 'regarding', taking due notice of the fact, III i 70; 'regarded in', looked on favourably by

REHEARSE, repeat, go over, III i 347; relate, IV i 26

RELISH, warble, sing happily

REMISSION, pardon

REMORSEFUL, compassionate

REPAIR, resort

REPEAL, recall (from banishment)

REPOSE, rely

REPUTE, 'how will the world repute me', what will people think of me?

RESORT (n.), company, III i 108; (v.) gathering, I ii 4; 'resort unto', visit

RESPECT, value, care about; 'respects friend', cares about friendship; 'in respect of her breath', by reason of her (bad) breath

RESPECTIVE, worthy of respect

REVOLT, turn traitor

RIFLE, rob

RIPE, mature

ROAD, harbour (Shakespeare treats both Verona and Milan, inaccurately, as seaports)

ROBIN HOOD'S FAT FRIAR, Friar Tuck

ROOT (n.), bottom (of the heart), V iv 103; (v.) allow to take root, II iv 158

SAD, serious, I iii 1

SADLY, sad

SAINT GREGORY'S WELL, (a real place near Milan)

SAINT NICHOLAS, (the patron saint of scholars)

SALT, 'cover of the salt', lid of the salt-cellar (often large and ornately decorated)

SALUTE, pay respects to

SAVE YOU, i.e. God save you (a common greeting)

SCANDALIZ'D, an object of scandal

SCARCE, scarcely

SCOURED, see WASHED AND SCOURED

SEAL, confirm, ratify, I iii 49

SEARCH, probe, cleanse (a surgical term)

SECRETS, see THRUST, III i 372

SEDGE, rush

SENSE, good sense (punning on 'senseless'), IV iv 194

SENSELESS, without feeling it, III i 143; insensible, incapable of feeling, IV iv 194

SEPULCHRE, bury

SEQUEL, what you were about to say

SERVANT, (a conventional description, in the language of courtly love, for a lady's acknowledged follower and admirer)

SERV'D ME, played on me

SERVE THE TURN, be good enough, do the job

SERVICE, (i.e. rescuing her from the outlaws), V iv 19

SERVICEABLE VOWS, vows of service (see SERVANT)

SET, (i) set to music, (ii) write, (iii) 'set store by', place importance on, I ii 81–2; 'set . . . at nought', care nothing for; 'set the world on wheels', take things easy (because his wife will earn money by her spinning; with a punning allusion to the spinning-wheel); sitting down (as opposed to 'standing affected'; with a pun on 'stand' = be sexually erect), II i 76

SEVERAL, separate, different

SHADOW, illusion, III i 178; (Shakespeare repeatedly plays on two senses of the word: (i) image, likeness (as opposed to reality), (ii) mere husk or shadow of a person), IV ii 120–6, IV iv 116, 193

SHALLOW, trivial (pun on the literal sense), I i 21; superficial, I ii 8; foolish, IV ii 92

SHAME, 'if shame lives . . . love', if there is any shame in a disguise adopted out of love
SHAPELESS, aimless, disorganised
SHAPES, appearances
SHARP, (i) the musical sense, (ii) painful (perhaps Julia has pinched or slapped her), I ii 91; keen, aggressive, III ii 67
SHE, she whom, III i 106
SHEEP, (punning on 'ship', which was pronounced the same way), I i 73
SHELVING, overhanging
SHIPP'D, embarked
SHOES, 'over shoes', up to the ankles (proverbial)
SHOT, tavern bill, II v 4, 7
SHOW, appear, II vii 48
SILLY, poor helpless, IV i 72
SINEWS, nerves (see also ORPHEUS)
SING, 'That I might sing it . . .' (the passage that follows, I ii 80–97, is an elaborate series of musical puns)
SIRRAH, fellow (a term of address to inferiors (used casually between equals at II v 8)
SITH, since
SLEEP, (punning on 'slip' = commit indecencies), III i 322
SLOW, heavy, sad, IV ii 62
SLUGGARDIZ'D, sunk in sloth
SO, (often) so long as; 'so you will sing it out' (i.e. don't change your mind and say you don't want the letter)
SO-HO, (a cry in hunting or hawking)
SOJOURN'D, stayed
SOLE, (punning on 'soul', with an allusion to the opinion of some theologians that women's souls were inferior to men's)
SOLEMNITY, festivities
SOLICIT, entreat
SOMETHING, somewhat, more or less
SORT, choose
SORTED WITH, in agreement with
SOUL-CONFIRMING, sworn on the soul
SOVEREIGN, having healing power, I ii 116
SPANIEL-LIKE, (the spaniel is proverbial for fawning loyalty even when beaten or mistreated)
SPEAKING, 'his little speaking', the fact that he says little
SPEED (v.), succeed, IV iv 103; 'be thy speed', assist you (with a pun on Speed's name)
SPITE, thing which causes pain
SPOKE, spoken
SPORT, playfulness
SQUIRREL, (i.e. dog no bigger than a squirrel)

STAND, halt, IV i 3; 'how stands the matter', what is the state of affairs; 'when it stands . . . with her', (i) when he is happy, so is she, (ii) when he has an erection, she is happy, II v 19–20; 'stand affected', see AFFECT
STARS, 'truer stars . . . birth', i.e. he was born under a conjunction of stars and planets which made his character honest and faithful (alluding to the astrological belief that character was determined by the position of the stars at birth)
STARV'D, nipped
STATE, state of affairs (see also PLEAD)
STATUE, (i.e. an idol to be worshipped)
STAY, delay, II ii 15; 'no more of stay', see NO
STAYS, is waiting (for)
STEAD, benefit, II i 102
STICK, slaughter (with a bawdy pun)
STILL, always, continually; 'love still', go on loving; 'still an end', continually, all the time
STOCK, (i) dowry, (ii) stocking, (iii) family, offspring (see also KNIT), III i 301–2; stocks (a device in which a person was fastened by the legs for public humiliation), IV iv 25
STOMACH, 'kill your stomach', (i) satisfy your appetite, (ii) vent your anger
STOOD IT NEXT TO DEATH, even to the point of death
STORE, supply
STRANGE, 'makes it strange', seems to be shocked or angry
STUDY, think about
SUBSCRIBE, 'To which . . . subscribe', I publicly acknowledge it (i.e. your 'unrivall'd merit') thus
SUBSTANCE, reality, real person (as opposed to 'shadow'), III ii 119, 122, IV iv 197
SUBTLE, crafty
SUCCESS, progress (not necessarily good), I i 58
SUCH ANOTHER, a similar
SUES TO, woos, is a suitor to
SUFFER, allow, I iii 5
SUGGESTED, tempted
SUM, total amount
SUIT, wooing
SUMMER-SWELLING, which grows in summer
SUN-EXPELLING MASK, (Elizabethan ladies often wore masks to protect their complexions from sunburn)
SURE, (often) certainly; safe, V i 12
SURFEIT, become sick from overeating

SWAIN, lover, V iv 12; 'swains', young men, IV ii 38

SWEET, (sometimes used as a term of address between male friends), II iv 150; 'sweet mouth', (i) sweet tooth, (ii) lecherous mouth; 'sweet-suggesting', sweetly tempting

SWING'D, beat, beaten

TABLE, notebook (often kept by Elizabethans as a record of private thoughts), II vii 3

TA'EN, taken, captured, III i 232

TAKE, 'anything to take to', any way of supporting yourself; 'takes upon him', claims, sets up

TAKE UP, (i) pick up, (ii) reprimand, I ii 134–5; (i) pick up, (ii) oppose, IV iv 193

TALE, (punning on 'tail' = posterior, a common vulgar joke), II iii 44–5

TANGLE, entangle, ensnare

TARRIANCE, delay

TARRY I HERE, if I stay here

TEMPER, mould

TENDER (adj.), (often) young; dear, V iv 37; (v.) have a tender concern for, feel sympathy for, IV iv 136; offer, V iv 76

TENOUR, 'The tenour . . . being', their general drift is merely to say that I am well and happy

TESTERN'D, gave a 'tester' or sixpence (one-seventh of a 'ducat')

TESTY, fretful

THAT, (often) so that; because, IV iv 60; what, III i 241; who, V ii 56; 'that you have about ye', what you have on you

THE GIFT THE GREATER, a greater gift

THENCE, from there

THERE, 'there . . . should love', I stop loving in the very situation where I ought to love (i.e. my love for Julia); 'there an end', that's the end of it

THEREBY, by means of which

THEREFORE, for that reason, IV i 60

THERETO, to this

THEREWITHAL, along with it, IV iv 81; by it, IV iv 166

THESEUS, see ARIADNE

THINK, 'think too much of', regard as excessive; 'To think upon', thinking about

THITHER, (to) there

THOUGHT, brooding, melancholy, I i 69; imagination, IV iv 168; 'thoughts', (i.e. Valentine's thoughts as expressed in his letters to Silvia), III i 140–9

THRIVE, be successful

THROUGHLY, thoroughly

THRUST HIMSELF INTO SECRETS, poke his nose into private affairs (with a bawdy double meaning)

THYSELF, (often) thou, you

TILTS AND TOURNAMENTS, (two forms of mock battle between mounted knights; a 'tilt' is between two single knights, a 'tournament' between two parties)

TIME, 'in good time', he arrives just at the right moment; 'of greater time', older

TIMELESS, untimely

TIRE, headdress

'TIS, there is, IV iv 62

TO, comparable to, II iv 135; over, II iv 149; compared to, II iv 162; as, III i 84; in opposition to, III i 223; to the accompaniment of, III ii 84, V iv 5; as to, IV ii 93; about, V ii 8; 'to leave', by leaving; 'to love me', in loving me; 'to it', get on with the job

TONGUES, knowledge of languages

TOOK UPON ME, assumed

TOUCH ME NEAR, are of great importance to me

TOURNAMENTS, see TILTS

TOYS, trifles

TRENCHED, cut

TRENCHER, plate

TRIFLE WITH, joke about (as she has done in the lines about 'my master' and 'my mistress')

TRIMM'D, dressed up

TRIUMPHS, processions, public shows

TRUE-DEVOTED, truly dedicated

TRUTH, (often) faithfulness, loyalty, honesty

TRY, test, III i 287; 'try me in', test me on

TUNE (v.), sing, III ii 85, V iv 6; 'Keep tune there', (i) stick to that tune, (ii) remain in that mood

TURN, change, be inconstant, II ii 4; 'turns me to shame', disgraces me; 'serve the turn', see SERVE

TWITS, reproaches

UNADVIS'D, thoughtlessly, carelessly

UNCIVIL, barbaric

UNDERSTANDS, (i) comprehends (Launce probably makes a gesture with his staff to illustrate his bawdy pun on 'stands'), (ii) stands under, supports, II v 25–6

UNDONE, ruined

UNGARTER'D, (going without garters (the bands holding up a man's 'hose' or stockings) was a traditional sign of lovesickness. Speed goes on to suggest that Valentine is in an even

worse state, since his hose themselves are (somehow) in disorder)
UNHEEDFUL, thoughtlessly made
UNJUST, false, treacherous
UNLESS THOU'DST TWO, unless you want to have two loyalties, i.e. to love me and Julia at the same time
UNMANNERLY, rude (with a pun on 'unmanly'?)
UNMELLOWED, not yet grey
UNPREVENTED, 'being unprevented', if the scheme is not forestalled
UNREVERENT, lacking reverence
UNSOUNDED, unfathomable
UNSTAID, improper, immodest
UNTUNEABLE, discordant
UNWIND, see BOTTOM
UP AND DOWN, exactly (with a pun on the movement of the shoe as he squeezes it up and down)
UPPER TOWER, i.e. the upper storey of a tower
URGE, put forward as an argument (for not doing it)
URINAL, a glass container used by doctors to examine urine
USE (n.), habitual practice, V iv 1; (v.) treat, IV iv 198–9, V iii 14

VAIN, useless, III i 168; foolish, IV iii 17
VALENTINE, (a traditional name for a lover, after St Valentine, patron saint of lovers); (i.e. a lover?), III i 191–2
VALENTINUS, (another form of 'Valentine')
VANISHED, (Launce's error for 'banished')
VANTAGE, 'false vantage', taking unfair advantage
VENGEANCE ON'T, (an oath: 'to hell with it!')
VERDURE, flourishing condition
VERONA, (presumably used here in error for 'Milan', but Shakespeare may have intended at one point to set the main action of the play in Verona. The play's geography is highly confused), III i 81, V iv 129
VERILY, truly
VERY, special, true, III ii 41
VICE, 'your old vice still', you always have the same bad habit
VISIT THEE WITH, inflict on you (joking)
VOTARY (TO), sworn follower (of)
VOUCHSAFE, grant

WAG, boy, lad

WAILFUL, full of laments
WAIT UPON, attend upon, III ii 96; 'wait upon his pleasure', am at his command
WANT, lack
WARRANT, 'warrant for', a guarantee of; 'upon this warrant', as a result of this authorisation
WASHED AND SCOURED, (punning on the senses 'knocked down' and 'beaten')
WATCH, stay awake at night
WATCHFUL, wakeful
WATER-SPANIEL, (a Treatise on English Dogs, published in 1576, lists the many clever things this type of hunting dog can be trained to do)
WAXED, grew
WEARY (v.), bore, II iv 122
WEDDING-DOW'R, dowry
WEED HER LOVE FROM VALENTINE, i.e. weed her love of Valentine out of the garden of her mind (?)
WEEDS, clothes
WELL-FAVOUR'D, 'Not so fair . . . as well-favour'd', i.e. her graciousness is even greater than her beauty; 'of you, well favour'd', well loved by you
WELL-REPUTED, of good reputation
WENCH, girl
WENT TO IT, died
WERE, (often) would be; would be suitable as, IV i 37
WHERE, whereas, III i 74; to a place where, IV ii 31; 'where to speak', to a place where I may speak, IV iv 105; 'where they're belov'd', those who love them in return
WHEREFORE, why
WHEREIN, during which, II ii 10; about which, III i 60
WHEREOF, of which
WHEREON, upon which
WHEREWITH, with which
WHITHER, (to) where; 'whither away', where are you going?
WHO, whoever, III i 77; he who, V iv 79
WHOLE, 'as whole as a fish', quite sound (a proverbial phrase of obscure origin)
WHORESON, (literally 'bastard', but an all-purpose derogatory adjective, like modern 'bloody')
WILD, (perhaps) open, unconfined, II vii 32
WILL (v.), want, II i 116; wish (see also COMPASS), IV ii 88–9; 'resolved will', determined willpower; 'what's your will', what do you want?

WINK, have one's eyes closed, I ii 139; close one's eyes, II iv 94, V ii 14

WIT, (often) intelligence, good sense; the mind, I i 35, 47, 69; 'he wants wit . . . better', the man lacks real intelligence whose will cannot teach his mind how to distinguish between good and bad (i.e. Proteus is denying the traditional doctrine that the reason should control the will, not vice versa)

WITH, by, II i 26; consistently with, II vii 6; by means of, III i 40

WITHAL, with it, II vii 67

WITHOUT, (a series of puns) (i) outside of, by the external appearance of, II i 30, 33, (ii) in the absence of, II i 31, (iii) unless, II i 32

WONDER, marvel at, V iv 169

WONT, accustomed

WOOD, (i) mad, (ii) wooden (with a pun on the wooden shoe), II iii 23

WORTHIES, excellences

WOT, know

WOULD, (often) wishes to, would like to; wish, II i 151, IV ii 62; wishes to go, IV iii 22; see NONE, II i 33; 'would I were . . . the same', i.e. I wish the letter still existed for me to be angry about it; 'I would have . . . one . . . to be', I think that . . . one . . . ought to be

WREATH YOUR ARMS, (folded arms were a conventional sign of sorrow or lovesickness)

WRIT, written

WRONG (n.), injury; (v.) injure; 'do him the more wrong', are very unfair to him

YET, up till now, III i 30

YOND, that, IV iv 62

YOUTH, young men, I i 2, IV iv 156